Good Housekeeping

LIGHT & HEALTHY

RECIPES

Jamaican Jerk Snapper with Grilled Pineapple (page 192)

Good Housekeeping
LIGHT & HEALTHY
RECIPES

HEARST BOOKS
A DIVISION OF STERLING PUBLISHING CO., INC.
NEW YORK

Rosemary Ellis **Editor in Chief**

Susan Westmoreland **Food Director**

Susan Deborah **Associate Food**
Goldsmith **Director**

Delia Hammock **Nutrition Director**

Sharon Franke **Food Appliances**
Director

Richard Eisenberg **Special Projects**
Director

Book Design by Renato Stanisic

The Library of Congress has catalogued the
2003 edition as follows:
Good Housekeeping light & healthy
cookbook: 375 delectable recipes for
everyday meals from the editors of Good
Housekeeping
      p. cm.
     ISBN 1-58816-271-0
     1. Cookery. 2. Low-fat diet--Recipes. I.
Title: Good Housekeeping
light and healthy cookbook. II. Good
Housekeeping Institute (New
York, N.Y.)
      TX714.G6496   2003
      641.5'638--dc21

2003006899

10 9 8 7 6 5 4 3 2 1

The Good Housekeeping Cookbook Seal
guarantees that the recipes in this cookbook
meet the strict standards of the Good
Housekeeping Research Institute, a source of
reliable information and a consumer advocate
since 1900. Every recipe has been triple-tested
for ease, reliability, and great taste.

Published by Hearst Books
A Division of Sterling Publishing Co., Inc.
387 Park Avenue South, New York, NY 10016

Good Housekeeping and Hearst Books are
trademarks of Hearst Communications, Inc.

www.goodhousekeeping.com

For information about custom editions, special
sales, premium and corporate purchases, please
contact Sterling Special Sales Department at
800-805-5489 or specialsales@sterlingpub.com.

Distributed in Canada by Sterling Publishing
c/o Canadian Manda Group, 165 Dufferin Street
Toronto, Ontario, Canada M6K 3H6

Distributed in Australia by Capricorn Link
(Australia) Pty. Ltd.
P.O. Box 704, Windsor, NSW 2756 Australia

Manufactured in China

Sterling ISBN 13: 978-1-58816-623-4
ISBN 10: 1-58816-623-6

CONTENTS

Bow Ties with Fennel and Leeks (page 111)

FOREWORD

Welcome to *Good Housekeeping*'s collection of Light & Healthy recipes.

We all want to eat nutritious meals. But sometimes it's hard finding easy, healthy recipes that everyone in your family will love. That's why we're so pleased to present this cookbook. Not only did we fill it with delicious recipes your family will want to eat, we created many dishes that are ready in less than 30 minutes to please the cook too.

The 150 entrees, appetizers, side dishes, and desserts in this book are sure to be crowd pleasers, whether you're making Tuesday night family dinner or entertaining friends on the weekend. Each has been triple tested by the pros in the *Good Housekeeping* kitchens, so you can be sure they'll come out great. We also offer dozens of terrific tips and shortcuts from our expert cooks to make your everyday food preparation easier.

You'll quickly discover that cooking with an eye towards good health doesn't mean sacrificing taste or familiar foods you know your family will eat. Roasted chicken, lasagna roll-ups, flatbread pizza and sinful desserts such as frozen chocolate mousse? Yes, all of these can be light and nutritious.

Happy, healthy cooking for you and your family!

—Susan Westmoreland
Food Director, *Good Housekeeping*

Southwestern Black-Bean Burgers (page 213)

INTRODUCTION

With You in Mind

Providing healthy, low-calorie meals that are satisfying and easy to prepare is a big concern for all of us today. As the relationship between diet and health hits the headlines repeatedly, we all want to do our best to produce meals for our families and ourselves that meet today's nutrition guidelines. But figuring out how to do it isn't always easy. The latest USDA Dietary Guidelines (www.health.gov/ Dietary Guidelines/) and My Pyramid Plan (www.MyPyramid.gov) have changed the rules, but the goal is the same. The specific suggestions have been revised based on current medical research and the presentation is different, but the intention is still to encourage us all to create a lifestyle that will lead to many years of good health.

Over the years, *Good Housekeeping* has been a trusted source for help in making the latest information on nutrition and health a part of your life. As the rules change, *GH* editors translate the underlying research and provide the tools you need to make it work for you. *Good Housekeeping Light & Healthy* follows that tradition by bringing you this collection of delicious, thoroughly tested recipes that meet today's dietary guidelines. The recipes emphasize more whole grains, more fruits and vegetables, more variety in the vegetables served, fat-free or reduced-fat dairy products, less sodium, and less saturated fat (with fat coming from healthy sources such as nuts, fish, and vegetable oils). In addition, from enticing appetizers through decadent desserts, the percentage of calories from fat in each recipe is less than 30 percent.

Calories Count

We hear a lot about America's nationwide weight gain and about the "flavor-of-the-day" diets that everyone is trying—but very little about counting calories. Calories aren't an old-fashioned enemy; they are simply a way of measuring the amount of energy produced when food is used by the body, and keeping an eye on them is still the most successful way to ease into a lifetime of weight control. Weight maintenance is just a matter of balance: Food calories in must equal energy calories out.

For centuries our bodies have been stocking up during times of plenty to insure survival during times of scarcity, so we are naturally programmed to tuck away all excess food calories as those potential energy calories we know as fat. And that is not likely to change any time soon. You might try the latest diet fad and enjoy momentary success, but pretty soon your body will think the famine it has been planning for has arrived and will steadfastly hang on to those stored calories in case things get worse. Lifetime weight maintenance requires setting reasonable weight goals for yourself and enjoying just enough of today's bounty to provide the energy you need for all you do. The nutrition information at the end of each recipe in *Good Housekeeping Light & Healthy* will help. Make balance a habit; go for healthy food that pleases you and exercise that is fun.

Also Important

While controlling the nutrient content of the recipes you prepare is a primary concern, providing mealtime satisfaction is also essential. A diet of healthy, low-calorie foods that aren't delicious and satisfying will soon be abandoned. If everyone is foraging for their favorite snack an hour after dinner, the plan has failed. The recipes you'll find in *Good Housekeeping Light & Healthy* have been tested and tasted in our kitchens with flavor and satiety in mind. We want you to discover how enjoyable healthy foods can be so you will want to make them a long-term part of your life.

And because we know there are many responsibilities competing for your time these days, as we developed recipes that are light and healthy, satisfying and delicious, we never forgot that quick and easy is also a plus

Climbing My Pyramid

For more than 65 years, the United States government has been offering nutrition guidelines in an effort to improve our health through diet. As new research changes the information available, these guidelines change: The USDA's latest Food Pyramid and Dietary Guidelines focus more attention on whole grains and exercise than ever before. The USDA also offers a fun, interactive web site where people can track their daily consumption and plan a diet that will take them in the right direction towards good nutrition.

The guidelines suggest that the ideal healthy diet is rich in whole grains, vegetables, fruits, and fat-free or reduced-fat dairy products. Healthy meals include lean meat, fish, and poultry, as well as beans, eggs,

and nuts, but limits saturated fats, trans fats, cholesterol, sodium, and added sugar. The new pyramid replaces the former horizontal blocks with colorful vertical bands and a staircase to remind us of the importance of exercise. Grains are represented by a large orange band, alongside vegetables in green, fruit in red, oils in yellow, milk in blue, and meat and beans in purple. The bands are of varying sizes, depending upon their importance in the new Dietary Guidelines. Recognizing that we all need a little fun in our lives, some Discretionary Calories have been bundled into the oils category.

While former guidelines recognized differences in dietary needs based on age and gender, the new plan also includes different levels of daily exercise. On the web site, www.mypyramid.gov, you can select your age, gender, and level of activity, then print out your personal dietary guidelines, complete with tips to help you achieve your goals. The site also offers a special area for children with an interactive video game, an area explaining each of the food groups, and areas for food professionals and teachers. For the ultimate dietary help, you can input your daily food and exercise record into My Pyramid Tracker and receive an in-depth assessment of how you are doing.

Organics: health food or hype?

Organic food seems like a healthy choice—even if the price is tough to swallow. But until recently, it was anyone's guess what "organic" really meant (regulation was local and hodgepodge). Now national standards are taking effect, and with them comes a new crop of groceries: organic everything, from mac & cheese to vanilla wafers. Should you pay more for these products (often produced by the same companies that make the regular versions)? In our taste tests of organics versus old standbys, many people didn't have a preference (suggesting that your decision probably won't be based on flavor). One standout: Of those who had a preference, 75 percent liked the original Oreo cookie better than its organic cousin. Here, more food for thought.

Why you would eat organic

To avoid artificial ingredients This includes synthetic colors and flavors, all prohibited by the new regulations.

To cut "bad" fats from your diet Artery-clogging partially hydrogenated oils are not allowed in organic food. Irradiated or genetically engineered ingredients also don't make the cut.

To limit exposure to pesticides Under the new rules, organic produce can't be treated with synthetic pesticides. But it's not pesticide free: There may be chemicals lingering in the soil or the air. A recent study found that organic foods contain a third of the residues present on conventional produce. Even so, the jury's still out on whether trace amounts of these substances are harmful to the consumer. Hormones, steroids, and antibiotics are also banned from organic meat, dairy, and poultry.

To protect the environment Organic farming reduces water contamination, improves soil quality, and protects wildlife habitats.

when you have to get dinner on the table after a busy day. The recipes that made the cut require very little hands-on time. They can either be prepared quickly and served, or mind themselves in the oven while you do other things.

We think a collection of easy and nutritious recipes that your family loves is worth a place in your kitchen and the healthy eating patterns that it encourages will become a family tradition. You'll see: *Light & Healthy* can be habit forming.

Easy Changes You Can Make Right Now

Enjoying a healthy lifestyle might require some changes, but they don't have to be painful. In fact, giving up your favorites forever should never be part of the program. There are actually a lot of small changes that will make a big step in the right direction. Here are ten of our favorites:

• Gradually switch to fat-free milk. You'll be amazed how easy it is to downsize from whole to fat-free milk if you do it in stages. Go to 2% for a few weeks, 1% for a while, and you are there. We'll bet you don't ever want to go back.

• Take control of salt. Watch out for hidden salt in seasonings such as spice mixtures and the seasoning packets that come with packaged foods. Look for brands that don't include salt and add only as much as you need.

• Break high-calorie combos. Discover bread with a little olive oil (instead of butter), baked potatoes with herbs (hold the sour cream), dessert without whipped cream (or ice cream)—you'll enjoy the food's flavor even more.

• Go whole grain. There are now more whole-grain choices than ever. Choose brown rice, whole-wheat pasta, and whole-grain breads. Be sure to check bread labels to see how much of the rich brown color actually comes from whole grains rather than from coloring agents, cocoa, or molasses.

• Snack from the produce department. Even if you are in a hurry, there are a lot of ready-to-eat fruit and vegetable choices in the produce department these days. If you don't see anything prepackaged that you want, go to the salad bar and select your own, just skip the dressing or choose a fat-free dressing and use it as a veggie dip.

Healthy Shopping

Healthy lifestyle changes start in the supermarket; if you make the right selections there, your time in the kitchen will be easy. Here are some strategies for filling your cart and your cupboards with light, healthy, and natural choices.

- Select recipes from *Good Housekeeping Light & Healthy* and make a list of healthy items you will need for the week's meals.
- Discard high-fat items from your cupboards and add low-fat versions of your favorites to the list.
- Add one item from the snack aisle to the list so you won't feel deprived; make it the small size.
- Head for the market, but not until you have a healthy breakfast, lunch, or dinner. If you aren't hungry, you're not as likely to be tempted by unhealthy choices.
- Buy just what you need; the large size isn't a bargain if it is more than you need.
- Check sell-by dates of groceries and select produce that is the freshest, even if it means tweaking a recipe or changing your menu.
- Compare nutrition facts labels among similar products and select those that best meet your dietary goals.
- Buy only what's on your list; don't be tempted by the end-of-aisle specials.
- Select the candy-free checkout lane; treat yourself to a magazine.

- Always read the nutrition facts labels. It doesn't take a lot of time and you can learn a lot. Sometimes those packages with the biggest fat-free, low-fat, or low-salt labels are very high in sugar and calories.

- Remember, liquid calories count. The number of calories in beverages might surprise you. Fruit juice, alcoholic drinks, milk, sweetened lemonade and iced tea, and soda all have more calories than you might expect. And, on a warm day, you might go ahead and have a refill. Just keep the calories in mind; you can always switch to water.

- Select soup. If you start a restaurant meal with even a cup of soup, you will feel satisfied faster and won't be tempted to order that high-calorie dessert. (Just make sure it's not a chowder or cream-based soup.) At home, a meal of soup makes a nutritious, yet low-calorie dinner.

• Explore reduced-fat, low-sodium options. Many reduced-fat and low-sodium products that will work well in your favorite family recipes. Grandma's lasagna might be just as delicious with reduced-fat cheeses and low-sodium tomatoes. In fact, she probably would have used them if they had been in her local market when she wanted, most of all, to produce healthy meals for her family.

• Walk to your local ice cream store or drive if it is really too far to walk—just don't keep that half-gallon in the freezer. You don't need to deny yourself your favorite treat, but if enjoying a bowl of ice cream requires a trip, you have to think about it and it becomes a special occasion.

APPETIZERS, SIDE DISHES & SALADS

Skewered Chicken with Papaya Salsa (page 25) and Sweet Pea Guacamole (page 23)

Backyard Bruschetta

Easy appetizers of grilled bread and your choice of two Italian-style toppings.

PREP: 15 MINUTES GRILL: 10 MINUTES MAKES 16 BRUSCHETTA.

TUSCAN WHITE BEAN TOPPING
(BELOW) OR TOMATO-GOAT CHEESE
TOPPING (PAGE 20)

1 loaf (8 ounces) Italian bread
2 garlic cloves, peeled and cut in half
1 tablespoon olive oil

1. Prepare one of the toppings; set aside.

2. Prepare grill. Cut off ends from bread; reserve for another use. Slice loaf diagonally into 1/2-inch-thick slices.

3. Place bread slices on grill over medium heat. Grill, turning occasionally, until lightly toasted, 8 to 10 minutes. Rub one side of each slice with cut side of garlic. Brush with oil.

4. Just before serving, assemble bruschetta by topping toast slices with either white bean topping, or goat cheese mixture and then tomato mixture.

Tuscan White Bean Topping

1 can (15 1/2 to 19 ounces) white
   kidney beans, rinsed and drained
1 tablespoon minced fresh parsley
   leaves
1 tablespoon lemon juice

1 tablespoon olive oil
1 teaspoon minced fresh sage leaves
2 1/4 teaspoons salt
1/8 teaspoon coarsely ground black
   pepper

In medium bowl, with fork, lightly mash beans, parsley, lemon juice, oil, sage, salt, and pepper until combined.

Each bruschetta with white bean topping: About 80 calories (23 percent calories from fat), 3g protein, 11g carbohydrate, 2g total fat (0g saturated), 0mg cholesterol, 175mg sodium.

Backyard Bruschetta

Tomato-Goat Cheese Topping

1 package (6 ounces) soft low-fat goat cheese

1 teaspoon minced fresh oregano leaves

1/4 teaspoon coarsely ground black pepper

2 ripe medium tomatoes, seeded and diced

2 teaspoons minced fresh parsley leaves

1 teaspoon olive oil

1/8 teaspoon salt

In small bowl, with fork, mix goat cheese, oregano, and pepper until blended. In medium bowl, mix tomatoes, parsley, oil, and salt.

Each bruschetta with goat cheese topping: About 70 calories (13 percent calories from fat), 3g protein, 7g carbohydrate, 1g total fat (0g saturated), 2mg cholesterol, 100mg sodium.

10 Guilt-Free Before-Dinner Snacks

- Celery stuffed with nonfat bean dip
- Dried fruit (apple rings, strawberries, cherries, cranberries, apricots, or raisins)
- Fat-free cinnamon-raisin bagel chips
- Fresh tangerine or Clementine sections
- Low-fat caramel or Cheddar rice cakes or popcorn cakes
- 1% or skim milk with chocolate syrup
- Pretzel sticks or whole-grain pretzels
- Red- or green-pepper strips, cucumber spears, or peeled baby carrots with salsa
- Reduced-fat mozzarella string cheese
- Toasted pita wedges with shredded reduced-fat cheese melted on top

Firecracker Mix

A spicy party snack so addictive, you can't eat just one handful! Omit the ground red pepper for kids or guests with a mild taste preference. Make up to a week in advance—store in ziptight plastic bags.

PREP: 10 MINUTES PLUS COOLING BAKE: 30 MINUTES PER BATCH
MAKES ABOUT 25 CUPS.

1/4 cup Worcestershire sauce
4 tablespoons butter or margarine
2 tablespoons brown sugar
1 1/2 teaspoons salt
1/2 to 1 teaspoon ground red pepper
  (cayenne)

12 cups popped corn (1/3 to 1/2 cup
  unpopped)
1 package (12 ounces) oven-toasted
  corn cereal squares
1 package (8 to 10 ounces) thin
  pretzel sticks

1. Preheat oven to 300°F. In 1-quart saucepan, stir Worcestershire, margarine, brown sugar, salt, and ground red pepper over low heat until margarine melts.

2. Place half each of popped corn, cereal, and pretzels in large roasting pan (17" by 11 1/2"); toss with half of Worcestershire mixture.

3. Bake popcorn mixture, stirring once halfway through baking, 30 minutes. Cool mixture in very large bowl or on counter covered with waxed paper. Repeat with remaining ingredients.

Each 1/2 cup: About 65 calories (14 percent calories from fat), 1g protein, 13g carbohydrate, 1g total fat (1g saturated), 3mg cholesterol, 242mg sodium.

Black Bean Dip

Simple to whip up—even when you're pressed for time. Serve with toasted pita points or crudités.

PREP: 5 MINUTES   COOK: 5 MINUTES   MAKES ABOUT 2 CUPS.

4 garlic cloves, peeled
1 can (15 to 19 ounces) black beans, rinsed and drained
2 tablespoons tomato paste
2 tablespoons olive oil
4 1/2 teaspoons fresh lime juice
1 tablespoon water
1/2 teaspoon ground cumin
1/2 teaspoon ground coriander
1/4 teaspoon salt
1/8 teaspoon ground red pepper (cayenne)

1. In 1-quart saucepan, place garlic and enough water to cover; heat to boiling over high heat. Reduce heat to low; cover and simmer 3 minutes to blanch garlic; drain.

2. In food processor with knife blade attached, puree garlic, beans, tomato paste, oil, lime juice, water, cumin, coriander, salt, and ground red pepper until smooth. Spoon dip into serving bowl; cover and refrigerate up to 2 days.

Each tablespoon: About 20 calories (45 percent calories from fat), 1g protein, 3g carbohydrate, 1g total fat (0g saturated), 0mg cholesterol, 55mg sodium.

Nutrition Spotlight: Beans

Beans are packed with protein and insoluble and soluble fiber. (Insoluble fiber helps promote regularity and may stave off such digestive disorders as diverticulosis. Soluble fiber can reduce blood cholesterol and help control blood-sugar levels in people with diabetes.) Beans are also high in saponin, a cancer-fighting plant compound.

Sweet Pea Guacamole

The perfect impostor: all the flavor and none of the fat found in traditional guacamole. Serve with baked tortilla chips for the full effect. See photo on page 16.

PREP: 10 MINUTES   MAKES ABOUT 3 CUPS.

2 packages (10 ounces each) frozen peas, thawed

3 tablespoons fat-free chicken or vegetable broth

2 tablespoons light mayonnaise

2 tablespoons fresh lime juice

2 tablespoons chopped fresh cilantro leaves

2 teaspoons chopped, seeded jalapeño chile

1/4 teaspoon ground cumin

1/4 teaspoon chili powder

salt to taste

chopped tomatoes and green onions for garnish

1. In food processor with knife blade attached, puree peas, broth, mayonnaise, lime juice, cilantro, jalapeño, cumin, chili powder, and salt until just smooth.

2. Spoon guacamole into serving bowl; garnish with tomatoes and green onions.

Each tablespoon: About 10 calories (0 calories from fat), 1g protein, 2g carbohydrate, 0g total fat, 0mg cholesterol, 30mg sodium.

Skewered Chicken with Papaya Salsa

Skewered Chicken with Papaya Salsa

These make the perfect light treat at a cocktail party. The refreshing papaya salsa can be prepared several days in advance and refrigerated until ready to use.

PREP: 30 MINUTES PLUS MARINATING   GRILL: 6 MINUTES
MAKES 10 APPETIZER SERVINGS.

2 tablespoons seasoned rice vinegar
   or balsamic vinegar
2 tablespoons Asian sesame oil
1 tablespoon fresh lemon juice
1 tablespoon reduced-sodium soy
   sauce
1 tablespoon hoisin sauce
1 teaspoon minced garlic
1 teaspoon minced, peeled fresh
   ginger
1 pound skinless, boneless chicken
   breast halves, cut into 1-inch cubes
6 (12-inch) bamboo skewers

PAPAYA SALSA
2 teaspoons olive oil
2 shallots, finely chopped
2 teaspoons minced, peeled fresh
   ginger
1/2 teaspoon curry powder
1 large ripe papaya, peeled, seeded,
   and finely chopped
2 tablespoons fresh lime juice
1 tablespoon finely chopped fresh
   cilantro leaves
salt to taste
lime wedges for garnish

1. In large ziptight plastic bag, combine vinegar, sesame oil, lemon juice, soy sauce, hoisin sauce, garlic, and ginger; add chicken, turning to coat. Seal bag, pressing out as much air as possible. Place bag on plate and re-frigerate 1 hour to marinate, turning occasionally. Soak skewers in water 20 minutes.

2. Meanwhile, prepare salsa: In nonstick 1-quart saucepan, heat olive oil over medium heat. Add shallots and ginger, and cook, stirring often, until softened, 6 to 7 minutes. Stir in curry powder; cook 1 minute. Transfer mixture to food processor with knife blade attached. Add papaya, lime juice, cilantro, and salt; pulse until just blended. Do not overprocess. Spoon salsa into bowl; serve at room temperature. If not serving right away, cover and refrigerate salsa up to 2 days. Bring to room temperature before serving. Makes about 2 cups.

3. Prepare grill. Thread chicken onto skewers without crowding. Place skewers on grill over medium heat and grill, turning occasionally, until chicken cubes lose their pink color throughout, 3 to 4 minutes a side. Arrange chicken skewers on platter; serve with salsa and lime wedges.

Each serving, chicken only: About 70 calories (26 calories from fat), 11g protein, 1g carbohydrate, 2g total fat (1g saturated), 29mg cholesterol, 65mg sodium.

Each 1/4 cup salsa: About 35 calories (26 percent calories from fat), 1g protein, 6g carbohydrate, 1g total fat (0g saturated), 0mg cholesterol, 75mg sodium.

Juicing a Lime

To get more juice from a lime, zap it whole in the microwave for 20 to 30 seconds. The juice flows more readily when the fruit is warm. Squeeze as you like, either with an electric citrus juicer for big jobs or an old-fashioned reamer for a few tablespoons.

Pickled Shrimp

Long a favorite in the Good Housekeeping dining room, this perfectly spiced appetizer is always made ahead: The shrimp are cooked the day before and marinated overnight. To keep them well chilled when served, set the bowl of shrimp in a larger bowl of crushed ice.

PREP: 20 MINUTES PLUS OVERNIGHT TO MARINATE   COOK: 5 MINUTES
MAKES 24 APPETIZER SERVINGS.

1/4 cup dry sherry
3 teaspoons salt
1/4 teaspoon whole black
  peppercorns
1 bay leaf
3 pounds large shrimp, shelled and
  deveined, leaving tail part of shell
  on, if desired

2/3 cup fresh lemon juice (about
  3 large lemons)
1/2 cup distilled white vinegar
1/2 cup vegetable oil
3 tablespoons pickling spices, tied in
  cheesecloth bag
2 teaspoons sugar
2 dill sprigs

1. In 4-quart saucepan, combine 6 cups water, sherry, 2 teaspoons salt, peppercorns, and bay leaf; heat to boiling over high heat. Add shrimp; heat to boiling. Shrimp should be opaque throughout when water returns to boil; if not, cook about 1 minute longer. Drain.

2. In large bowl, combine lemon juice, vinegar, oil, pickling spices, sugar, dill, and remaining 1 teaspoon salt. Add shrimp and toss well to coat. Spoon into ziptight plastic bags, press out excess air, and seal. Refrigerate shrimp overnight to marinate, turning bags occasionally.

3. Remove shrimp from marinade and arrange in chilled bowl. Serve with cocktail picks.

Each serving: About 69 calories (26 percent calories from fat), 9g protein, 1g carbohydrate, 2g total fat (0g saturated), 70mg cholesterol, 166mg sodium.

Mussels with Tomatoes and White Wine

This saucy dish should be served with plenty of good crusty bread for dipping.

PREP: 20 MINUTES   COOK: 25 MINUTES
MAKES 8 APPETIZER OR 4 MAIN-DISH SERVINGS.

1 tablespoon olive or vegetable oil
1 small onion, chopped
2 garlic cloves, finely chopped
1/4 teaspoon crushed red pepper
1 can (14 to 16 ounces) tomatoes

3/4 cup dry white wine
4 pounds large mussels, scrubbed
 and debearded
2 tablespoons chopped fresh parsley

1. In nonreactive 5-quart Dutch oven, heat oil over medium heat. Add onion and cook until tender and golden, 6 to 8 minutes. Add garlic and crushed red pepper and cook 30 seconds longer. Stir in tomatoes with their juice and wine, breaking up tomatoes with side of spoon. Heat to boiling; boil 3 minutes.

2. Add mussels; heat to boiling. Reduce heat; cover and simmer until mussels open, about 5 minutes, transferring mussels to large bowl as they open. Discard any mussels that do not open. Pour broth over mussels and sprinkle with parsley.

Each appetizer serving: About 104 calories (26 percent calories from fat), 9g protein, 6g carbohydrate, 3g total fat (1g saturated), 18mg cholesterol, 277mg sodium.

Mussels with Tomatoes and White Wine

Grilled Flatbread

This is an excellent accompaniment to any grilled meat or as a base for delicious toppings like Flatbread Salad Pizza (page 89).

PREP: 15 MINUTES PLUS DOUGH RISING AND RESTING
GRILL: 4 TO 6 MINUTES EACH   MAKES 12 APPETIZER SERVINGS.

1 package active dry yeast
1 teaspoon sugar
1¼ cups warm water (105° to 115° F)

about 4 cups all-purpose flour
about 3 tablespoons olive oil
2 teaspoons salt

1. In large bowl, combine yeast, sugar, and ¼ cup warm water; stir to dissolve. Let stand until foamy, about 5 minutes.

2. With wooden spoon, stir in 1½ cups flour, 2 tablespoons olive oil, salt, and remaining 1 cup warm water until combined. Gradually stir in 2 cups flour. With floured hand, knead mixture in bowl to combine.

3. Turn dough onto lightly floured surface and knead until smooth and elastic, about 10 minutes, working in more flour (about ½ cup), if necessary, to keep dough from sticking. Shape dough into ball and place in greased large bowl, turning dough to grease top. Cover bowl with plastic wrap and let rise in warm place (80° to 85°F) until doubled in volume, about 1 hour.

4. Punch down dough. Turn onto lightly floured surface; cover and let rest 15 minutes.

5. Grease two large cookie sheets. Shape dough into 4 balls. On lightly floured surface, with floured rolling pin, roll 1 ball at a time into a 12-inch round about ⅛-inch thick. Place rounds on prepared cookie sheets; lightly brush tops with some remaining oil.

6. Prepare outdoor grill for direct grilling over medium heat.

7. Place 1 round at a time, greased side down, on hot grill rack over medium heat and grill until grill marks appear on underside of dough and dough stiffens (dough may puff slightly), 2 to 3 minutes. Brush top with some remaining oil. With tongs, turn rounds over and grill until grill marks appear on underside and bread is cooked through, 2 to 3 minutes longer. Transfer flatbread to tray; keep warm. Repeat with remaining dough.

8. To serve, cut each flatbread into 6 wedges.

Each serving: About 185 calories (19 percent calories from fat), 5g protein, 32g carbohydrate, 4g total fat (1g saturated), 0mg cholesterol, 355mg sodium.

Zucchini and Sugar Snap Peas

PREP: 10 MINUTES   COOK: 10 MINUTES
MAKES 6 ACCOMPANIMENT SERVINGS.

1 tablespoon vegetable oil
3 medium zucchini (8 ounces each), cut into 1 1/2-inch chunks
1/2 pound sugar snap peas, stem and strings removed along both edges of each pea pod
2 green onions, cut into 1/2-inch pieces

1 tablespoon chopped fresh oregano or 1/2 teaspoon dried oregano leaves
3/4 teaspoon salt
1/4 teaspoon coarsely ground black pepper

Heat oil in nonstick 12-inch skillet over medium-high heat. Add the zucchini, snap peas, green onions, oregano, salt, and pepper. Cook, stirring frequently, until vegetables are golden and tender-crisp, 8 to 10 minutes.

Each serving: About 275 calories (13 percent calories from fat), 17g protein, 47g carbohydrate, 4g total fat (1g saturated), 0mg cholesterol, 295mg sodium.

Charred Peppers with Peaches

A welcome first course or side dish on its own, or as salad served on a bed of Boston or Bibb lettuce.

PREP: 30 MINUTES PLUS STANDING BROIL: 10 MINUTES
MAKES ABOUT 3 CUPS OR 4 ACCOMPANIMENT OR APPETIZER SERVINGS.

1 large yellow pepper
1 large red pepper
1 tablespoon olive oil
2 teaspoons fresh lemon juice
1/2 teaspoon ground cumin

1/4 teaspoon salt
1/8 teaspoon ground red pepper
  (cayenne)
3 large ripe peaches

1. Preheat broiler. Line broiling pan (without rack) with foil. Cut each pepper lengthwise in half; discard stem and seeds. Arrange peppers, cut side down, in broiling pan. With hand, flatten each pepper half. Place pan in broiler 5 to 6 inches from source of heat and broil peppers until skins are charred and blistered, about 10 minutes. Wrap foil around peppers and allow to steam at room temperature 15 minutes or until cool enough to handle.

2. Remove peppers from foil. Peel off skins and discard. Cut peppers lengthwise into 1/2-inch-wide strips. Pat dry with paper towels.

3. In bowl, mix peppers with olive oil, lemon juice, cumin, salt, and ground red pepper. Cover and refrigerate if not serving right away.

4. To serve, peel, pit, and slice peaches; stir into pepper mixture. Serve at room temperature.

Each serving: About 100 calories (27 percent calories from fat), 2g protein, 17g carbohydrate, 3g total fat (1g saturated), 0mg cholesterol, 135mg sodium.

Nutrition Spotlight: Red Peppers

Would it surprise you to learn that a half cup of red bell pepper has more vitamin C than a medium orange? Red peppers also contain flavonoids, which help enhance the potential benefits of vitamin C.

Charred Peppers with Peaches

Sautéed Cabbage with Peas

Onion, sautéed until golden, adds wonderful nutty flavor to this simple side dish.

PREP: 10 MINUTES   COOK: 25 MINUTES
MAKES ABOUT 6 CUPS OR 8 ACCOMPANIMENT SERVINGS.

2 tablespoons butter or margarine
1 medium onion, thinly sliced
1 small head savoy cabbage
   (2 pounds), tough outer leaves
   discarded, cored, and cut into
   1/2-inch-thick slices
3/4 teaspoon salt

1/2 teaspoon sugar
1/4 teaspoon coarsely ground black
   pepper
1/2 cup chicken broth
1 package (10 ounces) frozen
   baby peas
1/4 cup chopped fresh dill

1. In 12-inch skillet, melt margarine over medium heat. Add onion and cook, stirring often, until tender and golden, about 8 minutes.

2. Add cabbage, salt, sugar, and pepper; cook, stirring often, until cabbage is tender-crisp, about 5 minutes. Stir in broth, and cook until cabbage is tender, about 10 minutes.

3. Add frozen peas and dill. Cook over medium heat, stirring frequently, until heated through, about 5 minutes.

Each serving: About 90 calories (30 percent calories from fat), 4g protein, 13g carbohydrate, 3g total fat (2g saturated), 8mg cholesterol, 336mg sodium.

Nutrition Spotlight: Cruciferous Vegetables

Cabbage, brussels sprouts, bok choy, broccoli rabe, collard greens, and cauliflower have some cancer-prevention properties. Boosting your intake of these veggies will also provide you with plenty of fiber, vitamin C, and folate, a B vitamin that helps prevent birth defects and heart disease.

Microwave-Steamed Vegetables

Want fast, tasty vegetables? Follow these simple instructions and use the chart below to microwave-steam perfect veggies every time. And be sure to check out "12 Low-fat Ways to Dress Your Veggies" (page 41) for great sauces and flavor-boosters.

In a casserole dish, cook 1 pound vegetables (unless otherwise specified) with 1/4 cup water, covered, on high until tender, stirring halfway through cooking. Serve immediately.

VEGETABLE	MINUTES TO COOK
Asparagus	4 to 6
Beans, green or yellow wax	4 to 7
Beets, whole	10 to 14
Broccoli spears	5 to 6
Carrots, sliced	5 to 8
Cauliflower flowerets	5 to 6
Peas, shelled (1 cup)	4 to 5
Peppers, cut into strips	5 to 7
Spinach (10 ounces)	30 to 90 seconds
Vidalia onions (2), cut in half crosswise	7 to 8
Zucchini or yellow squash, sliced	4 to 7

Mixed Pea Pod Stir-Fry

Mixed Pea Pod Stir-Fry

This sweet and tender-crisp medley celebrates the glorious flavor of fresh green vegetables.

PREP: 15 MINUTES   COOK: 15 MINUTES
MAKES 4 ACCOMPANIMENT SERVINGS.

1 teaspoon salt
8 ounces green beans, trimmed
2 teaspoons vegetable oil
4 ounces snow peas, trimmed and
  strings removed

4 ounces sugar snap peas, trimmed
  and strings removed
1 garlic clove, finely chopped
1 tablespoon soy sauce

1. In 12-inch skillet, combine 4 cups water and salt; heat to boiling over high heat. Add green beans and cook 3 minutes. Drain; wipe skillet dry with paper towels.

2. In same skillet, heat oil over high heat. Add green beans and cook, stirring frequently (stir-frying), until they begin to brown, 2 to 3 minutes. Add snow peas, sugar snap peas, and garlic; stir-fry until snow peas and sugar snap peas are tender-crisp, about 1 minute longer. Stir in soy sauce and remove from heat.

Each serving: About 63 calories (29 percent calories from fat), 3g protein, 8g carbohydrate, 2g total fat (0g saturated), 0mg cholesterol, 844mg sodium.

Peas and Fava Beans

If you make this with fresh fava beans you'll have an extraordinary dish, but the frozen beans are almost as tasty.

PREP: 30 MINUTES PLUS COOLING   COOK: 12 MINUTES
MAKES 6 ACCOMPANIMENT SERVINGS.

4 1/2 pounds fresh fava beans or
  2 packages (10 ounces each)
  frozen baby lima beans
2 ounces pancetta or 2 slices bacon,
  chopped
1 garlic clove, thinly sliced

1 package (10 ounces) frozen baby
  peas, thawed
2 tablespoons chopped fresh parsley
1/4 teaspoon salt
1/8 teaspoon ground black pepper

1. Remove fava beans from shells and place in colander in sink. In 4-quart saucepan, heat 8 cups water to boiling over high heat. Pour boiling water over beans. When cool enough to handle, remove outer skins from fava beans. (If using lima beans, cook as label directs.)

2. In 10-inch skillet, cook pancetta and garlic over medium heat, stirring, until pancetta crisps, about 8 minutes.

3. Add peas, parsley, salt, and pepper and cook, stirring, 2 minutes. Add fava beans and cook, stirring, 2 minutes longer.

Each serving: About 149 calories (24 percent calories from fat), 10g protein, 19g carbohydrate, 4g total fat (1g saturated), 6mg cholesterol, 312mg sodium.

Peas and Fava Beans

Succotash

Corn and lima beans, two staples of Native American cooking, are combined to make this simple dish. The name succotash comes from the Narraganset word for "ear of corn."

PREP: 10 MINUTES   COOK: 25 MINUTES
MAKES 10 ACCOMPANIMENT SERVINGS.

5 slices bacon
3 stalks celery, cut into 1/4-inch-thick slices
1 medium onion, chopped
2 cans (15 1/4 to 16 ounces each) whole-kernel corn, drained
2 packages (10 ounces each) frozen baby lima beans

1/2 cup chicken broth
3/4 teaspoon salt
1/4 teaspoon coarsely ground black pepper
2 tablespoons chopped fresh parsley

1. In 12-inch skillet, cook bacon over medium-low heat until browned. With slotted spoon, transfer to paper towels to drain; crumble.
2. Discard all but 2 tablespoons bacon drippings from skillet. Add celery and onion and cook over medium heat, stirring, until vegetables are tender and golden, about 15 minutes. Stir in corn, frozen lima beans, broth, salt, and pepper; heat to boiling over high heat. Reduce heat; cover and simmer until heated through, 5 to 10 minutes longer. Stir in parsley and sprinkle with bacon.

Each serving: About 171 calories (26 percent calories from fat), 7g protein, 27g carbohydrate, 5g total fat (1g saturated), 5mg cholesterol, 458mg sodium.

12 Low-fat Ways to Dress Your Veggies

Boost the flavor—not the fat—with these simple alternatives to classic butter, cheese, and cream sauces.

- Make a mock hollandaise by mixing light mayonnaise with Dijon mustard, fresh lemon juice, and a pinch of ground red pepper. Drizzle cool sauce over steamed cauliflower, broccoli or—the classic partner— asparagus.
- Cook minced garlic and a pinch of red pepper flakes in a teaspoon of olive oil until fragrant. Add fresh spinach or Swiss chard to pan and cook until wilted.
- Toss chopped mixed fresh herbs (such as basil, mint, and oregano) and grated lemon zest with boiled potato halves.
- Heat chopped fresh tomato with crushed fennel seeds in a skillet until hot. Spoon over baked or broiled eggplant slices.
- Toast bread crumbs with chopped garlic in a teaspoon of olive oil. Sprinkle over steamed yellow squash with chopped parsley.
- Slice Canadian bacon (it's surprisingly low-fat) into thin strips and cook in a nonstick skillet until golden. Toss with steamed collard greens or spinach.
- Chop some mango chutney (available in the supermarket international or gourmet-food section) and mix into carrots or cauliflower.
- Thin orange marmalade with water and heat with ground ginger. Stir into hot green beans or broccoli.
- When steaming bitter greens like Swiss chard, add a handful of raisins for sweetness.
- Blend prepared horseradish, Dijon mustard, and light mayonnaise; drizzle over steamed green beans.
- Whisk together seasoned rice vinegar, soy sauce, and grated fresh ginger to taste. Use as a dipping sauce for tender-crisp broccoli.
- Flavor cooked green beans with a dusting of freshly grated Parmesan cheese (a little goes a long way) and crackled black pepper.

Roasted Beets and Red Onions

Roasting brings out and concentrates the natural sweetness in vegetables. In this recipe, beets and onions are roasted, then tossed with a simple balsamic sauce that enhances their rich flavors.

PREP: 20 MINUTES ROAST: 1 HOUR 30 MINUTES
MAKES ABOUT 4 CUPS OR 6 ACCOMPANIMENT SERVINGS.

2 pounds beets with tops (6 medium)	1 teaspoon dark brown sugar
3 small red onions (1 pound), unpeeled	1 teaspoon fresh thyme leaves
nonstick cooking spray	1/4 teaspoon salt
1/3 cup fat-free chicken broth	1/4 teaspoon coarsely ground black pepper
1/4 cup balsamic vinegar	finely chopped fresh parsley leaves

1. Trim tops from beets, leaving about 1 inch of stems attached. Scrub beets well under cold running water.

2. Preheat oven to 400°F. Place beets and unpeeled red onions in 10-inch oven-safe skillet or 13" by 9" metal baking pan. Coat vegetables lightly with nonstick cooking spray. Roast vegetables, shaking skillet occasionally, until onions are soft to the touch and beets are fork-tender, at least 1 hour and 30 minutes, depending on size of vegetables. (Beets may take longer than onions to roast; remove onions as they are done and continue roasting beets.)

3. Transfer vegetables to plate to cool slightly. Meanwhile, add broth, vinegar, brown sugar, and thyme to same skillet. Heat to boiling over high heat. Boil, stirring and scraping bottom of skillet, until liquid is dark brown and syrupy and reduced to about 1/4 cup, 5 to 7 minutes. Stir in salt and pepper. Remove skillet from heat.

4. Peel beets and onions when cool enough to handle. Cut beets into 2" by 1/4" matchstick strips and onions into thin rings; place in bowl. Pour reduced liquid over vegetables. Serve at room temperature, sprinkled with parsley.

Each serving: About 120 calories (0 calories from fat), 2g protein, 18g carbohydrate, 0g total fat, 0mg cholesterol, 195mg sodium.

Roasted Beets and Red Onions

Herbed Packet Potatoes

Potato chunks tossed with parsley and butter cook into tender morsels when wrapped in foil and baked.

PREP: 15 MINUTES   BAKE: 30 MINUTES
MAKES 6 ACCOMPANIMENT SERVINGS.

2 tablespoons butter or margarine
1 tablespoon chopped fresh parsley
1/2 teaspoon freshly grated lemon peel
1/2 teaspoon salt

1/8 teaspoon coarsely ground black pepper
1 1/2 pounds small red potatoes, cut in half

1. Preheat oven to 450°F. In 3-quart saucepan, melt butter with parsley, lemon peel, salt, and pepper over medium-low heat. Remove saucepan from heat; add potatoes and toss well to coat.

2. Place potato mixture in center of 24" by 18" sheet of heavy-duty foil. Fold edges over and pinch to seal tightly.

3. Place package in jelly-roll pan and bake until potatoes are tender when pierced (through foil) with knife, about 30 minutes.

Each serving: About 126 calories (29 percent calories from fat), 2g protein, 20g carbohydrate, 4g total fat (2g saturated), 10mg cholesterol, 241mg sodium.

Herbed Packet Potatoes

Reduced-Fat Macaroni and Cheese

They'll never know we took out ten grams of fat per serving, because this macaroni and cheese is as good as—even better than—the old-fashioned recipe.

PREP: 20 MINUTES   BAKE/BROIL: 22 MINUTES
MAKES 8 ACCOMPANIMENT OR 4 MAIN-DISH SERVINGS.

8 ounces elbow macaroni twists
1 container (16 ounces) low-fat cottage cheese (1%)
2 tablespoons all-purpose flour
2 cups fat-free (skim) milk
4 ounces sharp Cheddar cheese, shredded (1 cup)

1 teaspoon salt
1/4 teaspoon ground black pepper
pinch ground nutmeg
1/4 cup freshly grated Parmesan cheese

1. Preheat oven to 375°F. Grease broiler-safe, shallow 2 1/2-quart casserole. In medium saucepot, cook macaroni as label directs, but do not add salt to water. Drain.

2. In food processor with knife blade attached, puree cottage cheese until smooth. (Or, in blender, puree cottage cheese with 1/4 cup of milk in recipe until smooth.)

3. In 2-quart saucepan, blend flour with 1/4 cup milk until smooth. Slowly whisk in remaining milk until blended. Cook over medium heat, whisking, until mixture has thickened slightly and boils. Remove from heat; stir in cottage cheese, Cheddar, salt, pepper, and nutmeg.

4. Spoon macaroni into prepared casserole and cover with cheese sauce. Bake 20 minutes. Remove from oven; sprinkle with Parmesan. Turn oven control to broil.

5. Place casserole in broiler at closest position to heat source; broil until top is golden brown, 2 to 3 minutes.

Each main-dish serving: About 502 calories (25 percent calories from fat), 36g protein, 56g carbohydrate, 14g total fat (8g saturated), 42mg cholesterol, 1,448mg sodium.

Oven Fries

A quick way to make crispy "fries" without frying.

PREP: 10 MINUTES BAKE: 45 MINUTES
MAKES 4 ACCOMPANIMENT SERVINGS.

3 medium baking potatoes or sweet
  potatoes (8 ounces each), not
  peeled

1 tablespoon vegetable oil
1/2 teaspoon salt
1/8 teaspoon ground black pepper

1. Preheat oven to 425°F. Cut each potato lengthwise into quarters, then cut each quarter lengthwise into 3 wedges.

2. In jelly-roll pan, toss potatoes, oil, salt, and pepper to coat. Bake, turning occasionally, until tender, about 45 minutes.

Each serving: About 156 calories (23 percent calories from fat), 4g protein, 28g carbohydrate, 4g total fat (0g saturated), 0mg cholesterol, 301mg sodium.

Potato Pointers

Select potatoes that are firm and smooth. Avoid any with wrinkled skins, bruises, discolorations, or sprouts. Store the potatoes in a cool, dark place—but not in the refrigerator, where the starch converts to sugar and the nutrient value is reduced. Also important: Do not store potatoes with onions. Each vegetable releases a gas that hastens the spoilage of the other.

Gently scrub potatoes with a vegetable brush just before using; washing them in advance shortens their storage life. For even cooking, pick ones of uniform size. To prevent peeled potatoes from turning dark, toss with lemon juice.

Sauté of Potatoes, Tomatoes, and Fresh Corn

Accented with fresh tarragon and a lemony dressing, this simple side dish is perfect with steak.

PREP: 30 MINUTES   COOK: 40 MINUTES
MAKES ABOUT 12 CUPS OR 12 ACCOMPANIMENT SERVINGS.

4 tablespoons olive oil
2 pounds small red potatoes, cut into
  1-inch chunks
2 pints cherry tomatoes
4 cups corn kernels cut from cobs
  (about 8 ears)

2 teaspoons chopped fresh tarragon
  leaves
2 tablespoons fresh lemon juice
$^3/_4$ teaspoon salt
$^1/_4$ teaspoon coarsely ground black
  pepper

1. In nonstick 12-inch skillet, heat 1 tablespoon olive oil over medium heat. Add potato chunks and cook, stirring occasionally, until potatoes are browned on the outside and tender on the inside, about 35 minutes. Transfer potatoes to large bowl.

2. In same skillet, heat 1 more tablespoon oil; add whole cherry tomatoes and cook, stirring, 2 minutes. Add corn and tarragon, and cook 2 minutes longer. Transfer tomato mixture to bowl with potatoes.

3. In cup, mix lemon juice, salt, pepper, and remaining 2 tablespoons olive oil; pour over potato mixture and toss to combine.

Each serving: About 165 calories (27 percent calories from fat), 4g protein, 28g carbohydrate, 5g total fat (1g saturated), 0mg cholesterol, 150mg sodium.

Nutrition Spotlight: Sweet Corn

Sweet corn is one of the tastiest sources of folic acid. It's often mistakenly dismissed as a dieter's foe, but rest assured: One ear of fresh yellow or white corn has only 80 calories (if it's not slathered in butter, of course). Because its natural sugars start converting to starch as soon as it's picked, corn should be bought fresh and cooked the same day to preserve its sweetness.

Candied Sweet Potatoes

If there are marshmallow lovers in the family, top the already baked casserole with mini marshmallows and place in the oven for an extra 10 minutes. Do-ahead: This dish can be made through Step 1, covered, and refrigerated overnight. When ready to serve, continue with Steps 2 and 3.

PREP: 30 MINUTES   BAKE: 40 MINUTES
MAKES 12 ACCOMPANIMENT SERVINGS.

4 pounds sweet potatoes
  (8 medium), peeled and sliced
  into 1-inch-thick rounds
1/2 cup packed dark brown sugar
1/4 cup water

4 tablespoons butter or margarine
3/4 teaspoon salt
1/4 teaspoon coarsely ground black
  pepper
pinch nutmeg

1. In 6-quart saucepot, heat potatoes and enough water to cover to boiling over high heat. Reduce heat to low; cover and simmer until potatoes are barely fork-tender (slightly underdone), about 5 minutes. Drain well and place potatoes in shallow 2-quart casserole.

2. Preheat oven to 400°F. In 10-inch skillet, heat brown sugar, water, margarine, salt, pepper, and nutmeg over medium heat, stirring frequently, until margarine melts, about 3 minutes. Drizzle mixture evenly over potatoes.

3. Bake casserole, uncovered, basting potatoes occasionally with sugar mixture and turning slices over halfway through cooking, until potatoes are tender and lightly browned and sugar mixture thickens slightly, about 40 minutes.

Each serving: About 205 calories (18 percent calories from fat), 2g protein, 41g carbohydrate, 4g total fat (3g saturated), 10mg cholesterol, 193mg sodium.

Wild Rice and Orzo Pilaf

You can prepare this and refrigerate it for up to 2 days, then bake just before serving.

PREP: 25 MINUTES BAKE: 35 MINUTES
MAKES ABOUT 9 CUPS OR 12 ACCOMPANIMENT SERVINGS.

1 1/4 cups orzo pasta (8 ounces)
1 cup wild rice (6 ounces)
3 tablespoons butter or margarine
1 small onion, finely chopped
1 medium stalk celery, finely chopped
1 pound medium mushrooms,
   trimmed and sliced

2 teaspoons chopped fresh thyme
   leaves
1 teaspoon salt
1/4 teaspoon coarsely ground black
   pepper

1. Prepare orzo and wild rice, separately, as labels direct.
2. Meanwhile, in 12-inch skillet, melt margarine over medium heat. Add onion and celery, and cook, stirring occasionally, until tender, about 10 minutes. Add mushrooms, thyme, salt, and pepper; cook, stirring occasionally, until mushrooms are tender and liquid evaporates, about 10 minutes longer.
3. Preheat oven to 350°F. In shallow 2 1/2-quart baking dish, stir orzo, rice, and mushroom mixture until blended. Cover and bake until heated through, about 35 minutes.

Each serving: About 155 calories (17 percent calories from fat), 5g protein, 26g carbohydrate, 3g total fat (2g saturated), 8mg cholesterol, 211mg sodium.

Wheat Berry Pilaf

You'll love this veggie-flecked combination of nutty wheat berries and brown rice. Wheat berries are unmilled whole wheat kernels that have a delicious nutty, toasted flavor. Look for them in health-food stores and some supermarkets.

PREP: 30 MINUTES   COOK: 1 HOUR
MAKES ABOUT 8 CUPS OR 8 ACCOMPANIMENT SERVINGS.

1 cup wheat berries (whole-grain wheat)
1/2 cup long-grain brown rice
3 teaspoons olive oil
4 medium carrots, finely chopped
2 medium stalks celery, finely chopped
1 large onion, finely chopped
1 can (14 1/2 ounces) chicken broth or 1 3/4 cup homemade

1/2 pound green beans, trimmed and cut into 1 1/2-inch pieces
3/4 teaspoon salt
1/2 teaspoon freshly grated orange peel
1/4 teaspoon coarsely ground black pepper
1/4 teaspoon dried thyme
3/4 cup dried cranberries

1. In 3-quart saucepan, heat wheat berries and 4 cups water to boiling over high heat. Reduce heat to low; cover and simmer until wheat berries are firm to the bite but tender enough to eat, about 50 minutes. Drain and set aside.

2. Meanwhile, in 2-quart saucepan, prepare brown rice as label directs, but do not add butter or salt.

3. While wheat berries and brown rice are cooking, in deep 12-inch skillet, heat 2 teaspoons olive oil over medium heat. Add carrots and celery; cook, stirring occasionally, until almost tender, about 10 minutes. Add onion and remaining 1 teaspoon olive oil; cook, stirring occasionally, until vegetables are lightly browned, 12 to 15 minutes longer.

4. Increase heat to high; add broth, green beans, salt, orange peel, pepper, and thyme. Heat to boiling. Reduce heat to medium-high; cook, stirring often, until green beans are just tender, about 5 minutes.

5. Add cranberries, wheat berries, and brown rice to skillet, stirring to mix well; heat through.

Each serving: About 210 calories (13 percent calories from fat), 7g protein, 42g carbohydrate, 3g total fat (1g saturated), 0mg cholesterol, 395mg sodium.

SALADS

Watermelon and Jicama Salad

Jicama is a slightly flattened round root vegetable with a thin brown skin and crunchy white flesh.

PREP: 25 MINUTES PLUS CHILLING
MAKES ABOUT 8 CUPS OR 12 ACCOMPANIMENT SERVINGS.

2 medium jicama (12 ounces each), peeled and cut into 3/4-inch cubes
1/4 cup fresh lime juice (about 2 limes)
1/2 teaspoon salt
1 piece watermelon (2 1/2 pounds)

1/2 cup loosely packed fresh cilantro leaves, chopped
1/8 teaspoon ground red pepper (cayenne)
lime slices for garnish

1. In large bowl, toss jicama with lime juice and salt; cover and refrigerate 30 minutes.

2. Meanwhile, cut rind from watermelon and discard. Cut flesh into 1/2-inch cubes to equal 4 cups; discard seeds.

3. Add watermelon, cilantro, and ground red pepper to jicama in bowl; toss well. Cover and refrigerate 15 minutes to allow flavors to blend. Garnish with lime slices.

Each serving: About 40 calories (0 calories from fat), 1g protein, 9g carbohydrate, 0g total fat, 0mg cholesterol, 90mg sodium.

Watermelon and Jícama Salad

Peaches and Greens

A cool, refreshing alternative to a classic green salad.

Prep: 25 minutes Makes 12 accompaniment servings.

1 large lime
2 tablespoons honey
1 tablespoon olive oil
1 tablespoon chopped fresh mint
  leaves
1/2 teaspoon Dijon mustard
1/4 teaspoon salt
1/4 teaspoon coarsely ground black
  pepper

2 bunches watercress (4 ounces
  each), tough stems discarded
2 pounds ripe peaches (6 medium),
  peeled and cut into wedges
1 large jicama (1 1/4 pounds), peeled
  and cut into 1 1/2" by 1/4" sticks

1. From lime, grate 1/4 teaspoon peel and squeeze 2 tablespoons juice. Prepare dressing: In large bowl, with wire whisk, mix lime peel, lime juice, honey, oil, mint, mustard, salt, and pepper.

2. Just before serving, add watercress, peaches, and jicama to dressing in bowl; toss to coat.

Each serving: About 55 calories (16 percent calories from fat), 1g protein, 11g carbohydrate, 1g total fat (0g saturated), 0mg cholesterol, 55mg sodium.

Tomato and Melon Salad

PREP: 15 MINUTES   MAKES 8 ACCOMPANIMENT SERVINGS.

1 pint cherry tomatoes
1 large honeydew melon
   (4 1/2 pounds)
1 large cantaloupe (3 pounds)
1/4 cup red currant or apple jelly
1/2 teaspoon salt

1 teaspoon coarsely ground black
   pepper
1 bunch spinach, tough stems
   trimmed and washed and dried well

1. Cut small "x" in stem end of each cherry tomato. Add tomatoes to large saucepot of boiling water; cook 5 seconds. Drain; rinse tomatoes with cold running water to stop cooking. With fingers, slip tomatoes from their skins; place in colander to drain off excess liquid.

2. Cut each melon in half; discard seeds. With melon baller, scoop melons into balls; reserve any remaining melon for another use. Place melon balls in colander with cherry tomatoes. Cover colander, place on a plate to catch drips, and refrigerate if not serving right away.

3. To serve, in a large bowl, with wire whisk, stir jelly, salt, and pepper until smooth. Finely chop enough spinach to equal 1/4 cup. Add chopped spinach and melon-tomato mixture to bowl with jelly mixture; toss to coat. Arrange remaining spinach leaves on platter; spoon melon-tomato mixture over spinach leaves. Toss to serve.

Each serving: About 110 calories (8 percent calories from fat), 2g protein, 27g carbohydrate, 1g total fat (0g saturated), 0mg cholesterol, 190mg sodium.

Nutrition Spotlight: Tomatoes

Tomatoes are an excellent source of vitamin C, which enhances the body's ability to absorb iron. They also contain lycopene and other substances associated with lowering the risk of certain cancers.

Black-Eyed Pea Salad

Black-Eyed Pea Salad

Black-eyed peas, also called cowpeas, are actually beans. Unlike most dried beans, they don't need to be soaked. Their short cooking time makes them a natural for summer salads. Cayenne pepper sauce is a milder variety of hot pepper sauce that adds tang and flavor, not just heat. It can be found in the condiment section of the supermarket.

PREP: 15 MINUTES COOK: 30 MINUTES
MAKES 12 ACCOMPANIMENT SERVINGS.

1 package (16 ounces) dry black-eyed peas
1/3 cup cider vinegar
2 tablespoons olive oil
1 tablespoon cayenne pepper sauce
2 teaspoons sugar
1 1/2 teaspoons salt
2 medium stalks celery, finely chopped
1 medium red onion, finely chopped
1 package (10 ounces) frozen peas, thawed

1. Rinse black-eyed peas with cold running water and discard any stones or shriveled peas. In 8-quart Dutch oven, heat black-eyed peas and 3 quarts water to boiling over high heat. Reduce heat to low; cover and simmer until peas are just tender, 25 to 30 minutes.
2. Meanwhile, prepare dressing: In large bowl, with wire whisk, mix vinegar, oil, pepper sauce, sugar, and salt until blended.
3. Drain black-eyed peas and rinse well. Add warm black-eyed peas to dressing in bowl and toss gently. Stir in celery, onion, and peas. Serve salad at room temperature or cover and refrigerate until ready to serve.

Each serving: About 135 calories (20 percent calories from fat), 8g protein, 21g carbohydrate, 3g total fat (1g saturated), 0mg cholesterol, 360mg sodium.

Summer Corn Salad

A colorful salad created from farmstand-fresh summer vegetables.

PREP: 30 MINUTES COOK: 10 MINUTES
MAKES 12 ACCOMPANIMENT SERVINGS.

12 ears corn, husks and silk removed
12 ounces green beans, trimmed and
  cut into 1/4-inch pieces
1/2 cup cider vinegar
1/4 cup olive oil
1/4 cup chopped fresh parsley

1 teaspoon salt
1/2 teaspoon coarsely ground black
  pepper
1 red pepper, finely chopped
1 small sweet onion, such as Vidalia
  or Walla Walla, finely chopped

1. In 8-quart saucepot, heat 2 inches water to boiling over high heat; add corn. Heat to boiling. Reduce heat; cover and simmer 5 minutes. Drain. When cool enough to handle, cut kernels from corncobs.

2. Meanwhile, in 2-quart saucepan, heat 1 inch water to boiling over high heat; add green beans and heat to boiling. Reduce heat; simmer until tender-crisp, 3 to 5 minutes. Drain green beans. Rinse with cold running water; drain.

3. Prepare dressing: In large bowl, with wire whisk, mix vinegar, oil, parsley, salt, and black pepper until blended.

4. Add corn, green beans, red pepper, and onion to dressing in bowl; toss to coat. Serve at room temperature or cover and refrigerate up to 2 hours.

Each serving: About 179 calories (30 percent calories from fat), 5g protein, 31g carbohydrate, 6g total fat (1g saturated), 0mg cholesterol, 219mg sodium.

Sweet Onions

Sweet varieties of onions (such as Vidalia, Walla Walla, and Texas Spring Sweet) have a little less bite than regular onions. Be careful when you're storing sweet onions—they're more susceptible to bruising and nicks. All onions should be kept in a cool, dry environment that allows for adequate air circulation.

Barley Salad with Nectarines

Barley is another grain that makes a flavorful salad. You can use mangoes or peaches instead of the nectarines, if you prefer.

PREP: 30 MINUTES   COOK: 55 MINUTES
MAKES 16 ACCOMPANIMENT SERVINGS.

1 package (16 ounces) pearl barley
2 3/4 teaspoons salt
4 limes
1/3 cup olive oil
1 tablespoon sugar
3/4 teaspoon coarsely ground black pepper

1 1/2 pounds nectarines (4 medium), cut into 1/2-inch pieces
1 pound ripe tomatoes (2 large), seeded and cut into 1/2-inch pieces
4 green onions, thinly sliced
1/2 cup chopped fresh mint

1. In 4-quart saucepan, heat 6 cups water to boiling over high heat. Add barley and 1 1/2 teaspoons salt; heat to boiling. Reduce heat; cover and simmer until barley is tender and liquid has been absorbed, about 45 minutes. (Barley will have creamy consistency.)

2. Meanwhile, from limes, grate 1 tablespoon peel and squeeze 1/2 cup juice. Prepare dressing: In large bowl, with wire whisk, mix lime peel, lime juice, oil, sugar, pepper, and remaining 1 1/4 teaspoons salt until blended.

3. Rinse barley with cold running water; drain. Add barley, nectarines, tomatoes, green onions, and mint to dressing in bowl; stir gently until mixed and coated with dressing. Serve at room temperature or cover and refrigerate up to 1 hour.

Each serving: About 172 calories (26 percent calories from fat), 4g protein, 30g carbohydrate, 5g total fat (1g saturated), 0mg cholesterol, 333mg sodium.

Roasted Potato Salad

Potatoes and shallots, roasted until tender and caramelized, become a spectacular salad when tossed with a lemon-Dijon dressing.

PREP: 25 MINUTES   ROAST: 45 MINUTES
MAKES 6 ACCOMPANIMENT SERVINGS.

2 pounds red potatoes (12 medium), not peeled, cut into 1 1/2-inch pieces
16 small shallots, peeled, or 2 medium red onions, each cut into 8 wedges
1 teaspoon salt
1/4 teaspoon ground black pepper
2 tablespoons olive or vegetable oil
8 ounces French green beans (haricots verts) or regular green beans, trimmed
1 tablespoon fresh lemon juice
1 teaspoon Dijon mustard

1. Preheat oven to 425°F. In large roasting pan (17" by 11 1/2"), sprinkle potatoes and shallots with salt and pepper. Drizzle with 1 tablespoon oil and toss. Roast 30 minutes.

2. After vegetables have roasted 30 minutes, stir in green beans. Roast, stirring occasionally, until all vegetables are tender, about 15 minutes longer.

3. Meanwhile, prepare dressing: In large bowl, with wire whisk, mix lemon juice, remaining 1 tablespoon oil, and mustard until blended and smooth.

4. Add vegetables to dressing in bowl and toss to coat. Serve warm or at room temperature.

Each serving: About 212 calories (21 percent calories from fat), 5g protein, 39g carbohydrate, 5g total fat (1g saturated), 0mg cholesterol, 428mg sodium.

Roasted Potato Salad

Tomato and Mint Tabbouleh

Tabbouleh, the popular bulgur wheat and vegetable salad, is one of the best ways to enjoy tomatoes, cucumbers, and herbs.

PREP: 20 MINUTES PLUS STANDING AND CHILLING
MAKES 12 ACCOMPANIMENT SERVINGS.

1 1/2 cups boiling water
1 1/2 cups bulgur (cracked wheat)
1/4 cup fresh lemon juice
1 pound ripe tomatoes (3 medium), cut into 1/2-inch pieces
1 medium cucumber (8 ounces), peeled and cut into 1/2-inch pieces
3 green onions, chopped

3/4 cup loosely packed fresh flat-leaf parsley leaves, chopped
1/2 cup loosely packed fresh mint leaves, chopped
1 tablespoon olive oil
3/4 teaspoon salt
1/4 teaspoon coarsely ground black pepper

1. In medium bowl, combine water, bulgur, and lemon juice, stirring to mix. Let stand until liquid has been absorbed, about 30 minutes.

2. To bulgur mixture, add tomatoes, cucumber, green onions, parsley, mint, oil, salt, and pepper, stirring to mix. Cover and refrigerate to blend flavors, at least 1 hour or up to 4 hours.

Each serving: About 87 calories (21 percent calories from fat), 3g protein, 17g carbohydrate, 2g total fat (0g saturated), 0mg cholesterol, 157mg sodium.

Bulgur Wheat

This nutritious staple of the Middle East is a form of whole wheat kernels that has been boiled, dried, cracked, and sifted. Bulgur differs from cracked wheat in that it is precooked. Not only does bulgur contain soluble fiber, it is also a low-fat source of protein, vitamins, and minerals. It can be served hot or cold and it's quick and easy to prepare.

Tubetti Macaroni Salad

Carrots and celery add crunch to this lemon-scented salad. If the salad appears dry after chilling, stir in a touch of milk.

Prep: 25 minutes Cook: 25 minutes
Makes 12 accompaniment servings.

1 package (16 ounces) tubetti or
  ditalini pasta
2 3/4 teaspoons salt
4 carrots, peeled and cut into 2" by
  1/4" matchstick strips
1 to 2 lemons

2/3 cup light mayonnaise
1/3 cup milk
2 stalks celery, cut into 2" by 1/4"
  matchstick strips
2 green onions, thinly sliced

1. In large saucepot, cook pasta as label directs, using 2 teaspoons salt. After pasta has cooked 10 minutes, add carrots to pasta water and cook until carrots are just tender-crisp and pasta is done, 1 to 2 minutes longer.

2. Meanwhile, from lemon(s), grate 1 teaspoon peel and squeeze 3 tablespoons juice. Prepare dressing: In large bowl, with wire whisk, mix lemon peel, lemon juice, mayonnaise, milk, and remaining 3/4 teaspoon salt until blended.

3. Drain pasta and carrots; add to dressing in bowl, along with celery and green onions; toss until mixed and coated with dressing. Serve at room temperature or cover and refrigerate up to 4 hours.

Each serving: About 202 calories (22 percent calories from fat), 5g protein, 33g carbohydrate, 5g total fat (1g saturated), 5mg cholesterol, 463mg sodium.

SOUPS & SANDWICHES

Turkey and Mango Roll-Ups (page 84)

SOUPS

Cream of Asparagus Soup

Start with a package of frozen vegetables, a can of broth, and seasonings—in 25 minutes you'll have a luscious, creamy, lower-fat soup.

PREP: 5 MINUTES   COOK: 20 MINUTES
MAKES ABOUT 3 3/4 CUPS OR 4 FIRST-COURSE SERVINGS.

1 tablespoon butter or margarine
1 medium onion, finely chopped
1 can (14 1/2 ounces) fat-free chicken broth or 1 3/4 cups homemade
1 package (10 ounces) frozen asparagus cuts or spears
1/4 teaspoon dried thyme
1/4 teaspoon dried tarragon
1/8 teaspoon salt
1/8 teaspoon ground black pepper
1 1/2 cups fat-free (skim) milk
2 teaspoons fresh lemon juice
snipped fresh chives for garnish (optional)

1. In 2-quart saucepan, melt margarine over medium heat. Add onion and cook, stirring occasionally, until tender, 5 minutes. Add broth, asparagus, thyme, tarragon, salt, and pepper; heat to boiling over high heat. Reduce heat to low and simmer 10 minutes.
2. Spoon one-fourth of mixture into blender; cover, with center part of cover removed to let steam escape, and puree until smooth. Pour puree into bowl. Repeat with remaining mixture.
3. Return soup to saucepan; stir in milk. Heat through over medium heat, stirring often (do not boil, or soup may curdle). Remove saucepan from heat; stir in lemon juice. Garnish with snipped chives, if you like.

Each serving: About 115 calories (23 percent calories from fat), 8g protein, 11g carbohydrate, 3g total fat (2g saturated), 10mg cholesterol, 471mg sodium.

Cream of Lima Bean Soup

Prepare as directed but substitute 1 package (10 ounces) frozen lima beans for the asparagus. Delete the dried tarragon. If you like, garnish with chopped fresh thyme.

Each serving: About 155 calories (17 percent calories from fat), 9g protein,
20g carbohydrate, 3g total fat (2g saturated), 10mg cholesterol, 506mg sodium.

Cream of Kale Soup

Prepare as directed but substitute 1 package (10 ounces) frozen chopped kale for the asparagus. Add 1 garlic clove, minced, to the onions at the end of cooking time and cook 30 seconds longer. Omit the dried tarragon. Add the milk to the soup before pureeing. If you like, garnish with chopped fresh tomato.

Each serving: About 115 calories (23 percent calories from fat), 8g protein,
11g carbohydrate, 3g total fat (2g saturated), 10mg cholesterol, 471mg sodium.

Cream of Cauliflower Soup

Prepare as directed but substitute 1 package (10 ounces) frozen cauliflower florets for the asparagus and 1/2 teaspoon curry powder for the dried tarragon. If you like, garnish with chopped fresh apple.

Each serving: About 115 calories (23 percent calories from fat), 8g protein,
11g carbohydrate, 3g total fat (2g saturated), 10mg cholesterol, 471mg sodium.

Cream of Corn Soup

Prepare as directed but substitute 1 package (10 ounces) frozen whole-kernel corn for the asparagus. Add 3/4 teaspoon chili powder to the onions at the end of cooking time and cook 30 seconds longer. Omit the dried tarragon. If you like, garnish with chopped fresh cilantro.

Each serving: About 155 calories (17 percent calories from fat), 9g protein, 20g carbohydrate, 3g total fat (2g saturated), 10mg cholesterol, 506mg sodium.

Cream of Squash Soup

Prepare as directed but substitute 1 package (10 ounces) frozen winter squash for the asparagus. Add 1/4 teaspoon pumpkin-pie spice to the onions at the end of cooking time and cook 30 seconds longer. Omit the dried tarragon. If you like, garnish with chopped tomato.

Each serving: About 115 calories (23 percent calories from fat), 8g protein, 11g carbohydrate, 3g total fat (2g saturated), 10mg cholesterol, 471mg sodium.

Cream of Pea Soup

Prepare as directed but substitute 1 package (10 ounces) frozen peas for the asparagus. Substitute 1/4 teaspoon dried mint for the dried tarragon. If you like, garnish with nonfat yogurt.

Each serving: About 155 calories (17 percent calories from fat), 9g protein, 20g carbohydrate, 3g total fat (2g saturated), 10mg cholesterol, 506mg sodium.

Leek Consommé with Herbs

A simple yet elegant clear soup for a light start to a hearty meal.

PREP: 30 MINUTES COOK: 25 MINUTES
MAKES ABOUT 10 CUPS OR 10 FIRST-COURSE SERVINGS.

6 medium leeks (2 pounds)
2 medium stalks celery
4 medium carrots, peeled
1 lemon
3 cans (14 1/2 ounces each) chicken
  or vegetable broth or 5 1/4 cups
  homemade
3 cups water

1/8 teaspoon coarsely ground black
  pepper
1/4 cup loosely packed fresh parsley
  leaves, chopped
1 tablespoon coarsely chopped
  fresh dill
lemon slices for garnish

1. Cut root ends from leeks. Cut each leek crosswise to separate green tops from white bottoms, removing any tough outer leaves. Cut green tops crosswise into 1-inch pieces; place in large bowl of cold water. Use hands to swish leeks around to remove any grit or sand; repeat process, changing water several times. Drain well and place in 4-quart saucepan. Slice leek bottoms crosswise into thin slices; rinse thoroughly as with green tops and reserve separately.

2. Cut celery and 2 carrots crosswise into 1-inch chunks; thinly slice remaining 2 carrots crosswise on the diagonal. From lemon, with vegetable peeler, remove four 3" by 1" strips of peel; squeeze 1 tablespoon juice.

3. To saucepan with leek tops, add celery and carrot chunks, 2 strips lemon peel, broth, and water; heat to boiling over high heat. Reduce heat to low; cover and simmer 15 minutes.

4. Strain broth into 8-cup glass measuring cup or large bowl, pressing down on vegetables in strainer to extract as much broth as possible; discard vegetables. Return broth to saucepan.

5. Prepare consommé: Add pepper, lemon juice, leek bottoms, carrot slices, and remaining lemon peel to broth in saucepan; heat to boiling over high heat. Reduce heat to low; cover and simmer 10 minutes or just until vegetables are tender. Remove saucepan from heat; discard lemon peel. Stir in parsley and dill. Garnish each serving with a lemon slice.

Each serving: About 45 calories (20 percent calories from fat), 3g protein, 6g carbohydrate, 1g total fat (0g saturated), 1mg cholesterol, 405mg sodium.

Tomato and Rice Soup

Serve this old-fashioned comfort food with crusty bread and a tossed salad for a satisfying winter meal. If you can't find either Wehani (an aromatic, reddish-brown rice that splits slightly when cooked and has a chewy texture) or black Japonica (a dark rice that tastes like a cross between basmati and wild rice), you can use long-grain brown rice.

PREP: 20 MINUTES   COOK: 50 MINUTES
MAKES ABOUT 7 1/2 CUPS OR 8 FIRST-COURSE OR 4 MAIN-DISH SERVINGS.

1/2 cup Wehani, black Japonica, or long-grain brown rice
1 tablespoon butter or margarine
1 medium onion, finely chopped
1 medium stalk celery, finely chopped
1 medium carrot, peeled and finely chopped
1 garlic clove, crushed with garlic press
1/4 teaspoon dried thyme

1 can (28 ounces) plum tomatoes
1 can (14 1/2 ounces) chicken broth or 1 3/4 cups homemade
1 cup water
1/2 teaspoon salt
1/4 teaspoon coarsely ground black pepper
1 bay leaf
1/2 cup loosely packed fresh parsley leaves, chopped

1. Prepare rice as label directs but do not add salt, margarine, or butter; set rice aside.

2. Meanwhile, in 4-quart saucepan, melt margarine over medium heat. Add onion, celery, and carrot, and cook, stirring occasionally, until tender, about 10 minutes. Stir in garlic and thyme; cook 1 minute.

3. Add tomatoes with their juice, broth, water, salt, pepper, and the bay leaf; heat to boiling over high heat, breaking up tomatoes with side of spoon. Reduce heat to medium-low and cook, covered, 30 minutes. Discard bay leaf.

4. Spoon one-fourth of mixture into blender; cover, with center part of cover removed to let steam escape, and puree until almost smooth. Pour puree into bowl. Repeat with remaining mixture. Return soup to saucepan; heat over high heat until hot. Remove pan from heat; add cooked rice and chopped parsley.

Each first-course serving: About 95 calories (19 percent calories from fat), 3g protein, 16g carbohydrate, 2g total fat (2g saturated), 4mg cholesterol, 480mg sodium.

Tomato and Rice Soup

German Lentil Soup

German cooks like to add a meaty ham hock and some chopped bacon to their lentil soups to lend a smoky note.

PREP: 25 MINUTES   COOK: 1 HOUR 30 MINUTES
MAKES ABOUT 11 CUPS OR 6 MAIN-DISH SERVINGS.

4 slices bacon, cut into 1/2-inch pieces	1 smoked ham hock (1 pound)
2 medium onions, chopped	8 cups water
2 carrots, peeled and chopped	1 bay leaf
1 large stalk celery, chopped	1 teaspoon salt
1 package (16 ounces) lentils, rinsed and picked through	1/2 teaspoon dried thyme
	1/2 teaspoon ground black pepper
	2 tablespoons fresh lemon juice

1. In 5-quart Dutch oven, cook bacon over medium-low heat until lightly browned. Add onions, carrots, and celery; cook over medium heat until vegetables are tender, 15 to 20 minutes. Add lentils, ham hock, water, bay leaf, salt, thyme, and pepper; heat to boiling over high heat. Reduce heat; cover and simmer until lentils are tender, 50 to 60 minutes. Remove and discard bay leaf.

2. Transfer ham hock to cutting board. Cut meat into bite-size pieces, discarding skin and bone. Return meat to soup. Heat through. Stir in lemon juice.

Each serving: About 390 calories (23 percent calories from fat), 25g protein, 52g carbohydrate, 10g total fat (3g saturated), 13mg cholesterol, 1,027mg sodium.

The Skinny on Soup

Looking to lose a few pounds? Indulge in soup. Research shows that the best way to start a meal may be water- or broth-based soup. It fills you up—even more so than other foods low in calorie density. You'll feel full faster and end up eating less at that sitting. Or make a soup a meal in itself; with vegetable-based soups, you'll get plenty of fiber to keep you feeling full longer.

Curried Sweet-Potato and Lentil Soup

PREP: 15 MINUTES   COOK: 1 HOUR 15 MINUTES
MAKES ABOUT 14 CUPS OR 8 MAIN-DISH SERVINGS.

2 tablespoons butter or margarine
2 medium sweet potatoes
  (1 1/2 pounds), peeled and cut into
  1/2-inch chunks
2 large stalks celery, finely chopped
1 large onion, finely chopped
1 garlic clove, finely chopped
1 tablespoon curry powder
1 tablespoon grated, peeled fresh
  ginger
1 teaspoon ground cumin
1 teaspoon ground coriander

1 teaspoon salt
1/8 teaspoon ground red pepper
  (cayenne)
6 cups water
2 cans (14 1/2 ounces each)
  vegetable or chicken broth or
  3 1/2 cups homemade
1 package (16 ounces) dry lentils,
  rinsed and picked through
garnishes: yogurt, toasted coconut,
  and lime wedges (optional)

1. In 6-quart Dutch oven, melt margarine over medium heat. Add sweet potatoes, celery, and onion, and cook until onion is tender, about 10 minutes, stirring occasionally. Add garlic, curry powder, ginger, cumin, coriander, salt, and ground red pepper; cook, stirring, 1 minute.
2. To vegetables in Dutch oven, add water, broth, and lentils; heat to boiling over high heat. Reduce heat to low; cover and simmer, stirring occasionally, until lentils are tender, 40 to 45 minutes. Serve soup with yogurt, toasted coconut, and lime wedges if you like.

Each serving without garnishes: About 295 calories (12 percent calories from fat), 15g protein, 51g carbohydrate, 4g total fat (2g saturated), 8mg cholesterol, 646mg sodium.

Minestrone with Pesto

In Genoa, hearty minestrone is traditionally topped with a dollop of pesto.

PREP: 20 MINUTES PLUS SOAKING BEANS   COOK: 1 HOUR
MAKES 6 MAIN-DISH SERVINGS.

8 ounces dry Great Northern beans
(1 $1/3$ cups)
2 tablespoons olive oil
3 medium carrots, peeled and sliced
2 stalks celery, sliced
1 large onion, finely chopped
2 ounces sliced pancetta or bacon,
finely chopped
1 pound all-purpose potatoes
(2 large), peeled and cut into
$1/2$-inch cubes
1 pound zucchini (2 medium),
quartered length-wise then cut
crosswise into $1/4$-inch pieces

4 cups sliced savoy cabbage
($1/2$ medium head)
1 large garlic clove, crushed with
garlic press
2 cans (14 $1/2$ ounces each) chicken
broth or 3 $1/2$ cups homemade
1 can (14 $1/2$ ounces) diced
tomatoes
1 cup water
$1/2$ teaspoon salt
2 tablespoons pesto, homemade or
store-bought

1. Rinse beans under cold running water and discard any stones or shriveled beans. In large bowl, place beans and enough water to cover by 2 inches. Cover and let stand at room temperature overnight. (Or, in 4-quart saucepan, place beans and enough water to cover by 2 inches. Heat to boiling over high heat; cook 2 minutes. Remove from heat; cover and let stand 1 hour.) Drain and rinse beans.

2. In 4-quart saucepan, combine beans and enough water to cover by 2 inches; heat to boiling over high heat. Reduce heat to low; cover and simmer, stirring occasionally, until beans are tender, 40 minutes to 1 hour. Drain beans.

3. Meanwhile, in 5-quart Dutch oven, heat olive oil over medium-high heat. Add carrots, celery, onion, and pancetta; cook, stirring occasionally, until onion begins to brown, 10 minutes. Add potatoes, zucchini, cabbage, and garlic; cook, stirring constantly, until cabbage wilts. Add broth, tomatoes with their juice, and water; heat to boiling over high heat. Reduce heat to low; cover and simmer until vegetables are tender, about 30 minutes.

4. Spoon ¹/₂ cup beans and 1 cup soup into blender; cover, with center part of cover removed to let steam escape, and puree until smooth. Stir bean puree, remaining beans, and salt into soup; heat to boiling. Reduce heat to low; cover and simmer 10 minutes. Spoon soup into six soup bowls. Top each serving of soup with 1 teaspoon pesto.

Each serving: About 360 calories (28 percent calories from fat), 16g protein, 52g carbohydrate, 11g total fat (3g saturated), 6mg cholesterol, 1,100mg sodium.

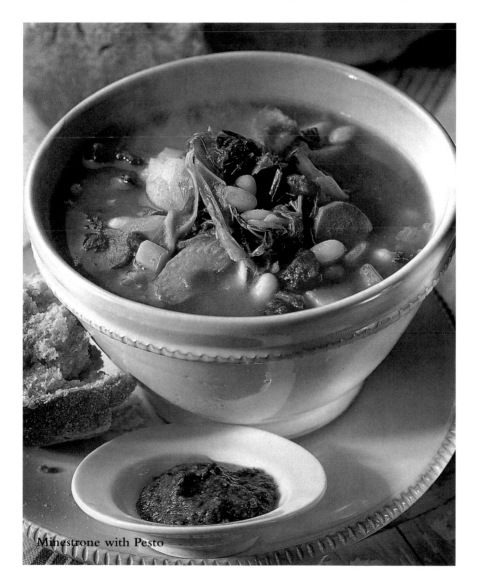

Minestrone with Pesto

Hearty Mushroom-Barley Soup

A real rib-sticker. Get a head start by cooking the barley the day before, then cool and refrigerate.

PREP: 20 MINUTES   COOK: 1 HOUR
MAKES ABOUT 12 CUPS OR 10 FIRST-COURSE SERVINGS.

3/4 cup pearl barley
8 cups water
2 tablespoons olive oil
3 stalks celery, cut into 1/4-inch-thick
   slices
1 large onion (12 ounces), chopped
1 1/2 pounds mushrooms, trimmed
   and thickly sliced

2 tablespoons tomato paste
5 carrots, each peeled and cut
   lengthwise in half, then crosswise
   into 1/4-inch-thick slices
2 cans (14 1/2 ounces each) beef
   broth or 3 1/2 cups homemade
1/4 cup dry sherry
1 1/2 teaspoons salt

1. In 3-quart saucepan, combine barley and 4 cups water; heat to boiling over high heat. Reduce heat; cover and simmer 30 minutes. Drain.
2. Meanwhile, in 5-quart Dutch oven, heat oil over medium-high heat. Add celery and onion; cook, stirring, until golden, about 10 minutes. Increase heat to high; add mushrooms and cook, stirring occasionally, until liquid has evaporated and mushrooms are lightly browned, 10 to 12 minutes.
3. Reduce heat to medium-high; add tomato paste and cook, stirring, 2 minutes. Add barley, carrots, broth, sherry, salt, and remaining 4 cups water; heat to boiling. Reduce heat; cover and simmer until carrots and barley are tender, 20 to 25 minutes.

Each serving: About 133 calories (27 percent calories from fat), 5g protein, 21g carbohydrate, 4g total fat (1g saturated), 1mg cholesterol, 684mg sodium.

Nutrition Spotlight: Barley

In most grains, the fiber is concentrated in the bran, which is removed when the kernel is refined. But even when all of barley's tough bran is removed (as with pearl barley, the most refined type), at least half of the original fiber remains. A half cup of cooked pearl barley contains 3 grams of fiber, compared to white rice's 1/3 gram.

Italian White Bean and Spinach Soup

A touch of fresh lemon juice, stirred in just before serving, gives this robust soup a light citrus note.

PREP: 20 MINUTES COOK: 30 MINUTES
MAKES ABOUT 7 1/2 CUPS OR 6 FIRST-COURSE SERVINGS.

1 tablespoon vegetable oil
1 medium onion, chopped
1 stalk celery, chopped
1 garlic clove, finely chopped
2 cans (15 to 19 ounces each) white kidney beans (cannellini), rinsed and drained
2 cups water
1 can (14 1/2 ounces) chicken broth or 1 3/4 cups homemade

1/4 teaspoon coarsely ground black pepper
1/8 teaspoon dried thyme
1 bunch (10 to 12 ounces) spinach, tough stems trimmed
1 tablespoon fresh lemon juice
freshly grated Parmesan cheese (optional)

1. In 3-quart saucepan, heat oil over medium heat. Add onion and celery; cook, stirring, until celery is tender, 5 to 8 minutes. Stir in garlic and cook 30 seconds. Add beans, water, broth, pepper, and thyme; heat to boiling over high heat. Reduce heat and simmer 15 minutes.

2. Roll up several spinach leaves together, cigar fashion, and thinly slice. Repeat with remaining spinach.

3. With slotted spoon, remove 2 cups beans from soup and reserve. Spoon one-fourth of remaining soup into blender; cover, with center part of cover removed to let steam escape, and puree until smooth. Pour into bowl. Repeat with remaining soup.

4. Return puree and reserved beans to saucepan; heat to boiling over medium-high heat. Stir in spinach and cook just until wilted, about 1 minute. Remove from heat and stir in lemon juice. Serve with Parmesan, if you like.

Each serving: About 170 calories (21 percent calories from fat), 11g protein, 24g carbohydrate, 4g total fat (1g saturated), 0mg cholesterol, 539mg sodium.

Caribbean Black-Bean Soup

Caribbean Black-Bean Soup

Our new take on black-bean soup is made with sweet potatoes and fresh cilantro for great flavor.

PREP: 45 MINUTES PLUS SOAKING BEANS COOK: 2 HOURS 30 MINUTES
MAKES ABOUT 13 CUPS OR 6 MAIN-DISH SERVINGS.

1 package (16 ounces) dry black beans
2 tablespoons vegetable oil
2 medium red onions, chopped
4 jalapeño chiles, seeded and minced
2 tablespoons minced, peeled fresh ginger
4 garlic cloves, finely chopped
1/2 teaspoon ground allspice
1/2 teaspoon dried thyme
8 cups water

1 1/2 pounds sweet potatoes (2 medium), peeled and cut into 3/4-inch chunks
1 tablespoon dark brown sugar
2 teaspoons salt
1 bunch green onions, thinly sliced
1 cup lightly packed fresh cilantro leaves, chopped
2 limes, cut into wedges (optional)

1. Rinse beans with cold running water and discard any stones or shriveled beans. In large bowl, place beans and enough water to cover by 2 inches. Cover and let stand at room temperature overnight. (Or, in 6-quart saucepot, place beans and enough water to cover by 2 inches. Heat to boiling over high heat; cook 2 minutes. Remove from heat; cover and let stand 1 hour.) Drain and rinse beans.

2. In 6-quart saucepot, heat vegetable oil over medium heat. Add onions and cook, stirring occasionally, until tender, about 10 minutes. Add jalapeño chiles, ginger, garlic, allspice, and thyme; cook, stirring, 3 minutes.

3. Add beans and water; heat to boiling over high heat. Reduce heat to low; cover and simmer 1 1/2 hours. Add sweet potatoes, brown sugar, and salt; heat to boiling over high heat. Reduce heat to low; cover and simmer until beans and sweet potatoes are tender, about 30 minutes longer.

4. Spoon 1 cup bean mixture into blender; cover, with center part of cover removed to let steam escape, and puree until smooth. Return to saucepot. Stir in green onions and cilantro. Serve with lime wedges, if you like.

Each serving: About 390 calories (14 percent calories from fat), 17g protein, 70g carbohydrate, 6g total fat (1g saturated), 0mg cholesterol, 705mg sodium.

Asian Chicken-Noodle Soup

Ours tastes just as good as, if not better than, any noodle-shop version.
Use chopsticks or a fork to pick up the long noodles.

PREP: 15 MINUTES   COOK: 35 MINUTES
MAKES ABOUT 7 CUPS OR 4 MAIN-DISH SERVINGS.

4 ounces rice noodles or linguine
3 cans (14 1/2 ounces each) chicken
   broth or 5 1/4 cups homemade
3/4 pound skinless boneless chicken
   breast halves
4 ounces shiitake mushrooms, stems
   removed and caps thinly sliced
2 tablespoons soy sauce

1 tablespoon grated, peeled fresh
   ginger
3/4 teaspoon salt
1/8 teaspoon crushed red pepper
1/4 teaspoon Asian sesame oil
1 cup loosely packed fresh cilantro
   leaves
2 green onions, thinly sliced

1. Prepare noodles as label directs; drain.

2. Meanwhile, in 4-quart saucepan, heat broth to boiling over high heat.
Add the chicken and reduce heat to low. Simmer until chicken is cooked
through, about 15 minutes. Remove chicken with a slotted spoon and set
aside to cool.

3. Stir mushrooms, soy sauce, ginger, salt, and crushed red pepper into
broth. Simmer, uncovered, 10 minutes.

4. Cut chicken into thin strips. Add chicken, sesame oil, and noodles to
broth and heat through. Stir in cilantro and green onions.

*Each serving: About 285 calories (16 percent calories from fat), 25g protein,
30g carbohydrate, 5g total fat (1g saturated), 58mg cholesterol, 1,050mg sodium.*

Asian Chicken-Noodle Soup

Beef and Barley Soup

One batch of this beef soup serves a party of eight. But we like to cook it over the weekend and freeze it in family-size portions for quick school-night dinners.

PREP: 45 MINUTES   COOK: 2 HOURS 30 MINUTES
MAKES ABOUT 16 CUPS OR 8 MAIN-DISH SERVINGS.

1 tablespoon plus 4 teaspoons
  vegetable oil
3 medium stalks celery, finely
  chopped
1 large onion, finely chopped
1 1/2 pounds lean boneless beef
  chuck, trimmed and cut into
  1/2-inch pieces
1/2 teaspoon salt
6 cups water
2 cans (14 1/2 ounces each) beef
  broth or 3 1/2 cups homemade
1 can (14 1/2 ounces) diced
  tomatoes

1 cup pearl barley
5 medium carrots (12 ounces),
  peeled and cut crosswise into
  1/4-inch-thick slices
5 medium parsnips (12 ounces),
  peeled and cut crosswise into
  1/4-inch-thick slices
2 medium turnips (8 ounces), peeled
  and finely chopped
3 strips (3" by 1" each) orange peel
pinch ground cloves

1. In 8-quart Dutch oven, heat 1 tablespoon vegetable oil over medium-high heat. Add celery and onion and cook, stirring occasionally, until tender and golden, about 10 minutes; transfer vegetables to bowl.

2. Pat beef dry with paper towels. In same Dutch oven, heat 2 teaspoons oil over high heat until very hot. Add half of beef and cook until browned on all sides. Transfer to plate. Repeat with remaining 2 teaspoons oil and beef.

3. Return beef to Dutch oven. Stir in salt, celery mixture, water, broth and tomatoes with their juice; heat to boiling over high heat. Reduce heat to low; cover and simmer 1 hour.

4. Add barley, carrots, parsnips, turnips, orange peel, and cloves; heat to boiling over high heat. Reduce heat to low; cover and simmer until beef, barley, and vegetables are tender, 50 to 60 minutes.

Each serving: About 320 calories (25 percent calories from fat), 25g protein, 36g carbohydrate, 9g total fat (3g saturated), 41mg cholesterol, 740mg sodium.

SANDWICHES

Roast Beef–Waldorf Club Sandwiches

Horseradish dressing and a crunchy celery-and-apple mixture make rare roast beef taste even better. Soaking in ice water crisps the onion and tames its bite.

PREP: 20 MINUTES PLUS STANDING MAKES 4 MAIN-DISH SERVINGS.

4 very thin slices red onion
1/2 Golden Delicious apple, peeled
    and finely chopped (1/2 cup)
2 stalks celery, finely chopped
4 tablespoons light mayonnaise
2 tablespoons sour cream
1/2 teaspoon fresh lemon juice

1 tablespoon bottled white
    horseradish
12 slices pumpernickel bread, lightly
    toasted if desired
8 ounces thinly sliced rare roast beef
1 bunch watercress (4 ounces),
    tough stems trimmed

1. In small bowl, combine onion with enough ice water to cover; let stand 15 minutes. Drain.

2. In separate small bowl, combine apple, celery, 2 tablespoons mayonnaise, 1 tablespoon sour cream, and lemon juice until well blended. In cup, combine remaining 2 tablespoons mayonnaise, remaining 1 tablespoon sour cream, and horseradish until blended.

3. Spread horseradish mixture evenly on 4 bread slices. Layer roast beef, onion, and watercress on top. Spread celery mixture evenly on 4 bread slices and place, celery mixture side up, over roast beef. Top with remaining bread slices. To serve, cut sandwiches in half.

Each serving: About 451 calories (30 percent calories from fat), 25g protein, 54g carbohydrate, 15g total fat (5g saturated), 50mg cholesterol, 842mg sodium.

Turkey and Mango Roll-Ups

A lime-spiked curried chutney adds zip to this rolled sandwich. If you can't find lavash (an Armenian flatbread), divide the filling ingredients among four 8- to 10-inch flour tortillas.

PREP: 25 MINUTES PLUS CHILLING MAKES 4 MAIN-DISH SERVINGS.

1 large lime
1/4 cup light mayonnaise
3 tablespoons mango chutney, chopped
1/2 teaspoon curry powder
1/8 teaspoon paprika
1 lavash flatbread (7 ounces)

1 medium cucumber (8 ounces), peeled and thinly sliced
8 ounces thinly sliced smoked turkey breast
1 medium mango, peeled and finely chopped
6 large green-leaf lettuce leaves

1. From lime, grate 1/4 teaspoon peel and squeeze 1 tablespoon juice. In bowl, combine lime peel, lime juice, mayonnaise, chutney, curry powder, and paprika until blended.

2. Unfold lavash; spread evenly with mayonnaise mixture. Arrange the cucumber slices over mayonnaise, then top with turkey, mango, and lettuce. From a short side, roll lavash up, jelly-roll fashion.

3. Wrap lavash roll in foil and refrigerate at least 2 hours or up to 4 hours to blend flavors and let bread soften. To serve, trim ends, then cut lavash roll into 4 pieces.

Each serving: About 375 calories (17 percent calories from fat), 18g protein, 55g carbohydrate, 7g total fat (2g saturated), 29mg cholesterol, 939mg sodium.

Cutting a Mango

With a sharp knife, cut a lengthwise slice from each side of the long flat seed, as close to the seed as possible. Peel the seed section and cut off as much flesh as possible; discard the seed. Cut the mango pieces lengthwise into thick wedges. Use a knife to remove the peel from each wedge, cutting close to the peel.

Turkey and Mango Roll-Ups

BBQ Pork Sandwiches

PREP: 10 MINUTES   BROIL: 15 MINUTES
MAKES 6 MAIN-DISH SERVINGS.

3 tablespoons light molasses
3 tablespoons ketchup
1 tablespoon Worcestershire sauce
1 teaspoon minced, peeled fresh
  ginger
1/2 teaspoon grated lemon peel

1 garlic clove, crushed with garlic
  press
2 whole pork tenderloins (3/4 pound
  each)
12 small, soft dinner rolls

1. Preheat broiler. In medium bowl, combine molasses, ketchup, Worcestershire, ginger, lemon peel, and garlic; add pork, turning to coat.
2. Place pork tenderloins on rack in broiling pan. Spoon any remaining molasses mixture over pork. Place pan in broiler 5 to 7 inches from heat source; broil pork, turning once, until meat is browned on the outside and still slightly pink in the center (internal temperature of tenderloins should be 160°F. on meat thermometer), 15 to 20 minutes.
3. To serve, thinly slice pork. Serve on rolls with any juices from broiling pan.

Each serving: About 390 calories (30 percent calories from fat), 32g protein, 35g carbohydrate, 13g total fat (4g saturated), 70mg cholesterol, 360mg sodium.

Whole Grains

The new Dietary Guidelines suggest that you make "half your grains whole." Whole grains include whole-wheat flour and anything made from it, as well as bulgur, rolled oats, whole cornmeal, brown rice, and barley. Refined grains include white flour and anything made from it, degermed cornmeal, and white rice. Although often enriched, refined grains still lack the fiber and trace minerals found in whole-grain products.

Chicken-Topped Pita Pizzas

PREP: 20 MINUTES BROIL: 2 MINUTES MAKES 6 MAIN-DISH SERVINGS.

2 teaspoons vegetable oil
1 medium red pepper, thinly sliced
1 medium green pepper, thinly sliced
1 medium onion, thinly sliced
3/4 cup bottled marinara sauce
1/4 teaspoon crushed red pepper
3 (6-inch) pitas

6 ounces smoked chicken, torn into
  fine shreds
1 cup shredded part-skim mozzarella
  cheese (4 ounces)
2 tablespoons sliced fresh basil
  leaves

1. In nonstick 12-inch skillet, heat oil over medium-high heat. Add red pepper, green pepper, and onion and cook until vegetables are tender-crisp. Stir in marinara sauce and crushed red pepper; heat through.

2. Preheat broiler. Split each pita horizontally into 2 halves. Place pita halves, split-side up, on cookie sheet. Place cookie sheet in broiler at closest position to heat source; broil pitas until lightly browned.

3. Spoon sauce on pita halves; top with chicken and mozzarella. Broil until cheese melts. Sprinkle with basil.

Each serving: About 215 calories (29 percent calories from fat), 14g protein, 25g carbohydrate, 7g total fat (3g saturated), 26mg cholesterol, 735mg sodium.

Flatbread Salad Pizza

 Soups & Sandwiches

Flatbread Salad Pizza

Try this salad pizza as an alternative to the usual tomato-and-cheese kind. It's especially good because it starts with our crusty Grilled Flatbread.

PREP: 20 MINUTES PLUS TIME TO PREPARE FLATBREAD

MAKES 8 FIRST-COURSE OR 4 MAIN-DISH SERVINGS.

GRILLED FLATBREAD (PAGE 30)
2 tablespoons extra virgin olive oil
2 tablespoons red wine vinegar
1 teaspoon sugar
1 teaspoon Dijon mustard
1/4 teaspoon salt
1/8 teaspoon coarsely ground black pepper

6 cups salad greens, such as radicchio, endive, and arugula, cut into 1/2-inch pieces
2 ripe medium tomatoes, cut into 1/2-inch pieces
1 small cucumber, peeled and cut into 1/2-inch pieces

1. Prepare Grilled Flatbread through step 5.

2. About 10 minutes before grilling flatbread, prepare salad: In large bowl, with wire whisk, mix oil, vinegar, sugar, mustard, salt, and pepper until dressing is blended.

3. Add salad greens, tomatoes, and cucumber to dressing in bowl; toss to coat well. Set salad aside.

4. Grill flatbreads as in step 6 of flatbread recipe.

5. To serve, top each flatbread with about 2 cups salad. Cut each round into quarters.

Each main-dish serving: About 620 calories (20 percent calories from fat), 16g protein, 106g carbohydrate, 14g total fat (2g saturated), 0mg cholesterol, 1,250mg sodium.

MAIN DISHES

Ziti with Roasted Asparagus (page 112)

SALADS

Tex-Mex Cobb Salad

Warm Southwestern accents give this classic a new attitude.

PREP: 30 MINUTES   MAKES 4 MAIN-DISH SERVINGS.

1/4 cup fresh lime juice

2 tablespoons chopped fresh cilantro leaves

4 teaspoons olive oil

1 teaspoon sugar

1/4 teaspoon ground cumin

1/4 teaspoon salt

1/4 teaspoon coarsely ground black pepper

1 medium head romaine lettuce (1 1/4 pounds), trimmed and leaves cut into 1/2-inch-wide strips

1 pint cherry tomatoes, each cut into quarters

12 ounces cooked skinless roast turkey meat, cut into 1/2-inch pieces (2 cups)

1 can (15 to 19 ounces) black beans, rinsed and drained

2 small cucumbers (6 ounces each), peeled, seeded, and cut into 1/2-inch-thick slices

1. Prepare dressing: In small bowl, with wire whisk, combine lime juice, cilantro, oil, sugar, cumin, salt, and pepper.

2. Place lettuce in large serving bowl. Arrange tomatoes, turkey, black beans, and cucumbers in rows over lettuce. Just before serving, toss salad with dressing.

Each serving: About 310 calories (20 percent calories from fat), 39g protein, 32g carbohydrate, 7g total fat (1g saturated), 71mg cholesterol, 505mg sodium.

Tex-Mex Cobb Salad

Couscous and Smoked-Turkey Salad

Couscous and Smoked-Turkey Salad

If you see plums, peaches, or apricots at the farmers' market, try using them instead of the nectarines.

PREP: 10 MINUTES   COOK: 5 MINUTES
MAKES 6 MAIN-DISH SERVINGS.

1 teaspoon ground cumin
1 package (10 ounces) couscous
   (Moroccan pasta)
1/3 cup dried tart cherries
3 tablespoons fresh lemon juice
2 tablespoons olive oil
1 tablespoon Dijon mustard
3/4 teaspoon salt

1/4 teaspoon coarsely ground black
   pepper
3 ripe medium nectarines, finely
   chopped
4 ounces smoked turkey breast
   (in 1 piece), cut into 1/4-inch pieces
Boston lettuce leaves

1. In 3-quart saucepan, heat cumin over medium-high heat until fragrant, 1 to 3 minutes. In saucepan with cumin, prepare couscous as label directs, adding cherries but no salt or butter.

2. Meanwhile, prepare dressing: In large bowl, with wire whisk or fork, mix lemon juice, oil, mustard, salt, and pepper until blended.

3. Stir warm couscous mixture, nectarines, and turkey into dressing in bowl. Spoon salad onto large platter lined with Boston lettuce leaves.

Each serving: About 300 calories (18 percent calories from fat), 11g protein, 51g carbohydrate, 6g total fat (1g saturated), 3mg cholesterol, 470mg sodium.

Couscous

Originally from North Africa, this grainlike pasta is made from semolina wheat flour. The packaged, precooked version is ready to eat in just five minutes and is widely available in supermarkets. Look for whole-wheat couscous which is very similar in taste and texture to regular couscous, but packs a whopping 8 grams of fiber.

Curried Chicken-Mango Salad

Precooked chicken from the deli or supermarket makes our salad a cinch. The recipe can easily be doubled if you need to feed a crowd.

PREP: 20 MINUTES   MAKES 4 MAIN-DISH SERVINGS.

1 store-bought rotisserie chicken (2 pounds)
1/4 cup plain low-fat yogurt
1/4 cup light mayonnaise
2 tablespoons mango chutney, chopped
1 tablespoon fresh lime juice
1 teaspoon curry powder
1 large ripe mango, peeled and finely chopped

1 medium stalk celery, finely chopped
1 medium Granny Smith apple, cored and finely chopped
1/2 cup loosely packed fresh cilantro leaves, chopped
1 head leaf lettuce, separated and rinsed

1. Remove skin from chicken; discard. With fingers, pull chicken meat into 1-inch pieces.

2. In large bowl, with wire whisk, mix yogurt, mayonnaise, chutney, lime juice, and curry powder until combined. Stir in chicken, mango, celery, apple, and cilantro until well coated. Serve salad on bed of lettuce leaves.

Each serving: About 310 calories (26 percent calories from fat), 32g protein, 25g carbohydrate, 9g total fat (2g saturated), 95mg cholesterol, 255mg sodium.

Curried Chicken-Mango Salad

Sesame Noodle and Chicken Salad

A great dish to make when you have leftover chicken.

PREP: 25 MINUTES   COOK: 15 MINUTES   MAKES 6 MAIN-DISH SERVINGS.

12 ounces linguine or spaghetti
6 ounces snow peas, strings removed
   and cut crosswise into thirds
3/4 cup very hot water
1/4 cup creamy peanut butter
3 tablespoons seasoned rice vinegar
3 tablespoons soy sauce
1 tablespoon light brown sugar
1 tablespoon minced, peeled fresh
   ginger
1 tablespoon Asian sesame oil

1/4 teaspoon ground red pepper
   (cayenne)
1 small garlic clove, crushed with
   garlic press
2 medium carrots, peeled and
   shredded
3 cups thinly sliced red cabbage
   (1/2 small head)
12 ounces boneless, roasted chicken,
   pulled into thin strips

1. In large saucepot, cook pasta as label directs. During last minute of pasta cooking, add snow peas. Continue cooking until pasta is done. Drain linguine and snow peas. Rinse under cold running water to cool; drain again and set aside.

2. Meanwhile, prepare dressing: In large bowl, with wire whisk, mix hot water, peanut butter, rice vinegar, soy sauce, brown sugar, ginger, sesame oil, ground red pepper, and garlic until blended.

3. Add pasta, snow peas, carrots, red cabbage, and chicken to dressing in bowl; toss to blend.

Each serving: About 460 calories (25 percent calories from fat), 28g protein, 58g carbohydrate, 13g total fat (3g saturated), 51mg cholesterol, 880mg sodium.

Warm Pork Tenderloin Salad with Dijon Dressing

PREP: 20 MINUTES COOK: 5 MINUTES MAKES 4 MAIN-DISH SERVINGS.

1 pork tenderloin (12 ounces), well trimmed

2 tablespoons dry sherry

1 tablespoon plus 1 1/2 teaspoons soy sauce

2 teaspoons grated, peeled fresh ginger

2 tablespoons light mayonnaise

2 tablespoons balsamic vinegar

1 tablespoon water

1 tablespoon Dijon mustard with seeds

1 teaspoon sugar

1/4 teaspoon coarsely ground black pepper

2 large heads Belgian endive, cut crosswise into 1-inch-thick slices

1 small head radicchio, thinly sliced

2 bunches arugula (8 ounces), stems trimmed

1 package (10 ounces) frozen peas, thawed

1. Holding knife almost parallel to the cutting surface, slice pork crosswise into very thin slices. In bowl, mix pork, sherry, soy sauce, and ginger; set aside.

2. In large bowl, with wire whisk, stir mayonnaise, vinegar, water, mustard, sugar, and pepper until blended. Add endive, radicchio, and arugula; toss well.

3. Spray nonstick 12-inch skillet lightly with nonstick cooking spray. Heat skillet over medium-high heat. Add pork mixture to skillet and cook, stirring quickly and constantly, until pork just loses its pink color, about 2 minutes.

4. Add pork and peas to salad; toss well.

Each serving: About 230 calories (27 percent calories from fat), 24g protein, 17g carbohydrate, 7g total fat (2g saturated), 45mg cholesterol, 270mg sodium.

PASTA

Bow Ties with a Trio of Peas

Snow peas, sugar snap peas, and green peas are combined in a lemon broth to make this a simple yet elegant pasta dish.

PREP: 15 MINUTES   COOK: 25 MINUTES   MAKES 4 MAIN-DISH SERVINGS.

1 package (16 ounces) bow-tie or rotini pasta
1 tablespoon butter or margarine
1 tablespoon olive oil
4 ounces snow peas, strings removed
4 ounces sugar snap peas, strings removed
1 garlic clove, crushed with garlic press

1 cup frozen baby peas
1/2 cup low-sodium chicken or vegetable broth
3/4 teaspoon salt
1/4 teaspoon coarsely ground black pepper
1/2 teaspoon freshly grated lemon peel

1. In large saucepot, cook pasta as label directs. Drain and keep warm.
2. Meanwhile, in 10-inch skillet, melt butter with oil over medium-high heat. Add snow peas and sugar snap peas and cook, stirring, until tender-crisp, 1 to 2 minutes. Stir in garlic and cook 30 seconds. Add frozen baby peas, broth, salt, and pepper; heat to boiling. Stir in lemon peel. In warm serving bowl, toss pasta with vegetable mixture until combined.

Each serving: About 536 calories (13 percent calories from fat), 19g protein, 95g carbohydrate, 8g total fat (3g saturated), 8mg cholesterol, 704mg sodium.

Penne with Spinach and Raisins

Golden raisins add an unexpected touch of sweetness.

PREP: 15 MINUTES   COOK: 20 MINUTES   MAKES 6 MAIN-DISH SERVINGS.

1 package (16 ounces) penne pasta
3 tablespoons olive oil
4 garlic cloves, crushed with side of
  chef's knife
1 bunch (10 to 12 ounces) spinach,
  tough stems trimmed, washed and
  dried very well

1 can (15 to 19 ounces) garbanzo
  beans, rinsed and drained
1/2 cup golden raisins
1/2 teaspoon salt
1/4 teaspoon crushed red pepper
1/2 cup chicken or vegetable broth

1. In large saucepot, cook pasta as label directs. Drain and keep warm.
2. Meanwhile, in 12-inch skillet, heat oil over medium heat. Add garlic and cook until golden. Increase heat to medium-high. Add spinach, beans, raisins, salt, and crushed red pepper; cook, stirring frequently, just until spinach wilts. Stir in broth and heat through.
3. In warm serving bowl, toss pasta with spinach mixture.

Each serving: About 445 calories (20 percent calories from fat), 14g protein, 76g carbohydrate, 10g total fat (1g saturated), 0mg cholesterol, 466mg sodium.

Pairing Pastas with Sauces

Not every pasta works with every sauce. Here's a general guide to using the most common shapes:

Long *(spaghetti, vermicelli, linguine, spaghetti, capellini [angel hair]):* Best with smooth tomato- and oil-based sauces; save ultra-thin capellini for light sauces or use in broths.

Long Straws *(perciatelli, bucatini):* Ideal for pesto, cheese, or creams sauces.

Short *(farfalle [bow ties], fusilli [corkscrews], orecchiette [little ears], shells, gemelli, radiatore):* Serve with butter, cheese, tomato, meat, vegetable, and light oil-based sauces; they catch every drop.

Short Tubes *(penne, rigatoni, ziti):* Bite for bite, the most suitable partner for meat, vegetable, and chunky tomato sauces.

Small *(pastina, ditalini, orzo, stelline, tubettini):* Use in broths or soups.

Wide *(tagliatelle, fettuccine, pappardelle, lasagna, mafalda):* Substantial enough to support cream, cheese, and thick meat sauces.

Orzo "Risotto" with Mushrooms

Orzo "Risotto" with Mushrooms

PREP: 10 MINUTES COOK: 20 MINUTES MAKES 6 MAIN-DISH SERVINGS.

1 package (16 ounces) orzo pasta
1 tablespoon olive oil
1 medium onion, chopped
8 ounces medium shiitake
  mushrooms, stems removed and
  caps cut into 1/4-inch-thick slices
8 ounces medium white mushrooms,
  trimmed and cut into 1/4-inch-thick
  slices
1/2 teaspoon salt
1/4 cup dry white wine
2 tablespoons cornstarch
2 1/2 cups low-fat milk (1%)
1/3 cup grated Parmesan cheese
3 tablespoons chopped fresh parsley
  leaves
1 tablespoon butter or margarine

1. In 5-quart saucepot, cook orzo as label directs; drain and keep warm.

2. Meanwhile, in nonstick 12-inch skillet, heat oil over medium heat. Add onion and cook 5 minutes. Increase heat to medium–high. Add shiitake and white mushrooms and 1/4 teaspoon salt; cook, stirring frequently, until mushrooms are tender and golden. Remove skillet from heat; stir in white wine.

3. In small bowl, mix cornstarch with milk. Add cornstarch mixture to same 5-quart saucepot. Heat to boiling over medium heat. Reduce heat to low; simmer 1 minute. Stir in orzo, mushroom mixture, grated Parmesan, parsley, margarine, and remaining 1/4 teaspoon salt; heat through. Serve "risotto" immediately while still creamy.

Each serving: About 425 calories (17 percent calories from fat), 17g protein, 70g carbohydrate, 8g total fat (3g saturated), 13mg cholesterol, 609mg sodium.

Nutrition Spotlight: Mushrooms

Mushrooms contain two powerful antioxidants—the plant compound quercetin and the mineral selenium. Quercetin may reduce blood-clot formation, and selenium, in combination with vitamin E, protects cells from free-radical damage that may lead to heart disease and cancer.

Linguine with Fresh Tomato Sauce

If the ripe summer tomatoes you use taste a bit acidic, simply add one teaspoon sugar to the sauce. If using juicy beefsteak tomatoes instead of meaty plum tomatoes, simmer the sauce uncovered for about twenty minutes to allow the excess juices to evaporate.

PREP: 15 MINUTES   COOK: 30 MINUTES   MAKES 6 MAIN-DISH SERVINGS.

1 tablespoon olive oil
1 small onion, chopped
2 pounds ripe plum tomatoes or beefsteak tomatoes, peeled and coarsely chopped
1/2 teaspoon salt

3 tablespoons butter, cut into pieces, or olive oil
2 tablespoons chopped fresh sage or 1/2 cup chopped fresh basil
1 package (16 ounces) linguine or penne

1. In nonstick 10-inch skillet, heat oil over medium heat. Add onion and cook until tender and golden, about 10 minutes. Add tomatoes and salt; heat to boiling over high heat. Reduce heat; cover and simmer, stirring and breaking up tomatoes with side of spoon, until sauce has thickened, 15 to 20 minutes. Stir in butter and sage.
2. Meanwhile, in large saucepot, cook pasta as label directs. Drain. In warm serving bowl, toss pasta with sauce.

Each serving: About 388 calories (23 percent calories from fat), 11g protein, 65g carbohydrate, 10g total fat (4g saturated), 16mg cholesterol, 334mg sodium.

Penne with Tomato Cream

This restaurant favorite is a cinch to prepare at home. Don't hesitate to add the vodka. You won't taste it: It just melds the flavors.

PREP: 15 MINUTES   COOK: 30 MINUTES   MAKES 6 MAIN-DISH SERVINGS.

1 tablespoon olive oil
1 small onion, chopped
1 garlic clove, finely chopped
1/8 to 1/4 teaspoon crushed red pepper
1 can (28 ounces) tomatoes in puree, coarsely chopped
3 tablespoons vodka (optional)

1/2 teaspoon salt
1/2 cup heavy or whipping cream
1 cup frozen peas, thawed
1 package (16 ounces) penne or rotini pasta
1/2 cup loosely packed fresh basil leaves, thinly sliced

1. In nonstick 12-inch skillet, heat oil over medium heat. Add onion and cook until tender, about 5 minutes. Add garlic and crushed red pepper; cook until garlic is golden, about 30 seconds longer. Stir in tomatoes with their puree, vodka if using, and salt; heat to boiling over high heat. Reduce heat and simmer until sauce has thickened, 15 to 20 minutes. Stir in cream and peas; heat to boiling.
2. Meanwhile, in large saucepot, cook pasta as label directs. Drain. In warm serving bowl, toss pasta with sauce and sprinkle with basil.

Each serving: About 434 calories (23 percent calories from fat), 13g protein, 71g carbohydrate, 11g total fat (5g saturated), 27mg cholesterol, 509mg sodium.

White vs. Whole-Wheat Pasta

Enriched brands of whole-wheat pasta have more thiamin, riboflavin, and folic acid than regular pasta and contain about five times the amount of fiber. And the nutty taste of whole wheat makes it a great choice for fall and winter cooking. Whole wheat spaghetti, made with whole wheat flour, delivers more fiber per 2-ounce serving (5 grams versus 2 grams).

Pasta Primavera

Pasta Primavera

This dish is traditionally made in spring, when the first tender young vegetables appear   thus the name *primavera*, which means spring in Italian. We used fresh asparagus and sugar snaps and cooked them along with the pasta to save time.

PREP: 15 MINUTES   COOK: 25 MINUTES   MAKES 6 MAIN-DISH SERVINGS.

1/2 cup heavy or whipping cream
3 tablespoons butter or margarine
4 ounces shiitake mushrooms, stems removed and caps thinly sliced
2 very small yellow squash or zucchini (4 ounces each), cut into 2" by 1/4" matchstick strips
4 green onions, thinly sliced
1 tablespoon chopped fresh parsley

1 package (16 ounces) fettuccine
1 pound asparagus, trimmed and cut on diagonal into 1 1/2-inch pieces
4 ounces sugar snap peas, strings removed
3/4 cup freshly grated Parmesan cheese
1/4 teaspoon salt

1. In 1-quart saucepan, heat cream to boiling and boil 1 minute. Remove saucepan from heat and set aside.

2. In nonstick 10-inch skillet, melt butter or margarine over medium heat. Add mushrooms and cook, stirring, 1 minute. Add squash and cook, stirring, until vegetables are tender, about 3 minutes. Remove from heat; stir in green onions and parsley. Keep warm.

3. Meanwhile, in large saucepot, cook pasta as label directs. After pasta has cooked 7 minutes, add asparagus and sugar snap peas to pasta water. Cook until pasta and vegetables are tender, 3 to 5 minutes longer. Drain pasta and vegetables, reserving 1/2 cup pasta cooking water.

4. In warm serving bowl, toss pasta and vegetables with reserved pasta water, Parmesan, and salt. Stir in cream and mushroom mixture.

Each serving: About 491 calories, 18g protein, 64g carbohydrate, 18g total fat (11g saturated), 52mg cholesterol, 462mg sodium.

Bow Ties with Cannellini and Spinach

PREP: 10 MINUTES   COOK: 15 MINUTES   MAKES 4 MAIN-DISH SERVINGS.

12 ounces bow-tie pasta

2 bags (10 ounces each) prewashed spinach

1 tablespoon olive oil

1 jumbo onion (1 pound), thinly sliced

3/4 cup chicken or vegetable broth

1 teaspoon cornstarch

1/2 teaspoon salt

1/4 teaspoon crushed red pepper

1 can (15 to 19 ounces) white kidney beans (cannellini), rinsed and drained

2 tablespoons grated Pecorino Romano or Parmesan cheese

1. In large saucepot, cook pasta as label directs. Just before draining pasta, stir spinach into water in saucepot; leave in only until it wilts. Drain pasta and spinach; return to saucepot and keep warm.

2. Meanwhile, in nonstick 12-inch skillet, heat oil over medium-high heat. Add onion and cook until golden brown, 10 to 12 minutes. In 1-cup glass measuring cup, mix broth, cornstarch, salt, and crushed red pepper. Add to skillet along with beans and cook over medium-high heat until sauce boils and thickens slightly, about 1 minute.

3. Add sauce to pasta and spinach in saucepot; toss to mix well. Sprinkle with Romano to serve.

Each serving: About 545 calories (12 percent calories from fat), 24g protein, 99g carbohydrate, 7g total fat (1g saturated), 5mg cholesterol, 925mg sodium.

Nutrition Spotlight: Green Leafy Vegetables

Spinach, swiss chard, parsley, basil, and arugula contain magnesium—a mineral essential for bone health and muscle contraction—and potassium, which helps regulate blood pressure. They also supply certain carotenoids that may lower the risk of macular degeneration.

Bow Ties with Cannellini and Spinach

Bow Ties with Fennel and Leeks

Bow Ties with Fennel and Leeks

The vegetables become sweet and tender when cooked in olive oil.

PREP: 35 MINUTES BAKE: 20 MINUTES MAKES 6 MAIN-DISH SERVINGS.

4 medium leeks (1 1/2 pounds)
2 tablespoons olive oil
2 medium fennel bulbs (1 pound each), trimmed and thinly sliced, feathery tops reserved
2 garlic cloves, finely chopped
1 tablespoon sugar
1 package (16 ounces) bow-tie or gemelli pasta

1 cup chicken or vegetable broth
1/4 cup heavy or whipping cream
1/2 cup grated Parmesan cheese
1/2 teaspoon salt
1/4 teaspoon coarsely ground black pepper
1 ripe, medium tomato, finely chopped

1. Preheat oven to 400°F. Cut off root ends and tough green tops from leeks. Cut each leek lengthwise in half, then crosswise into 1/4-inch-wide slices. Place in large bowl of cold water. Use hands to swish leeks around to remove any grit or sand. Repeat process, changing water several times. Drain well.

2. In nonstick 12-inch skillet, heat 1 tablespoon oil over medium heat. Add leeks and cook, stirring frequently, until tender and golden, about 15 minutes. Add fennel, garlic, sugar, and remaining 1 tablespoon oil; cook, stirring frequently, until fennel is tender and light golden, about 20 minutes.

3. Meanwhile, cook pasta as label directs. Drain; return pasta to saucepot and keep warm.

4. When fennel is tender, add broth, cream, all but 2 tablespoons Parmesan, salt, and pepper; boil 1 minute.

5. Spoon pasta into deep 4-quart casserole. Add leek mixture and toss well. Sprinkle top with chopped tomato and remaining 2 tablespoons Parmesan. Cover and bake until hot and bubbly, about 20 minutes. Garnish with fennel tops to serve.

Each serving: About 460 calories (22 percent calories from fat), 15g protein, 77g carbohydrate, 11g total fat (4g saturated), 17mg cholesterol, 560mg sodium.

Ziti with Roasted Asparagus

Toasted pecans make this easy dish luxurious.

PREP: 15 MINUTES   ROAST/COOK: 30 MINUTES
MAKES 6 MAIN-DISH SERVINGS.

2 tablespoons olive oil
1/4 teaspoon dried rosemary
2 pounds asparagus, trimmed and cut
   into 1-inch pieces (6 cups)
1 package (16 ounces) ziti pasta
1 cup half-and-half or light cream

3/4 teaspoon freshly grated
   lemon peel
1/2 teaspoon salt
1/4 teaspoon ground black pepper
1/3 cup toasted pecans, coarsely
   chopped

1. Preheat oven to 400°F. Combine oil and rosemary in 13" by 9" baking pan. Place pan in oven until oil is hot, about 4 minutes. Add asparagus; toss to coat with oil. Roast asparagus, tossing occasionally, until tender, about 15 minutes.

2. Meanwhile, in large saucepot, cook the pasta as label directs. Drain.

3. In 12-inch skillet, heat half-and-half to boiling over medium heat; cook 5 minutes. Stir in lemon peel, salt, and pepper. Add pasta and asparagus; toss to coat. Transfer to warm serving bowls and sprinkle with pecans.

Each serving: About 410 calories (26 percent calories from fat), 15g protein, 63g carbohydrate, 12g total fat (4g saturated), 15mg cholesterol, 282mg sodium.

Nutrition Spotlight: Asparagus

Fresh asparagus is a springtime treat not to be missed. It's a great source of folic acid, which protects against birth defects (in women of childbearing years) and heart disease. Enjoy it with rich salmon, or steam up a big handful (it takes less than 10 minutes), sprinkle lightly with salt or a pinch of grated Parmesan cheese, and enjoy. At 3 calories a spear, you can afford to eat the whole bunch.

Ziti with Roasted Asparagus

Lasagna Roll-Ups

Lasagna Roll-Ups

PREP: 35 MINUTES   BAKE: 35 MINUTES
MAKES 6 MAIN-DISH SERVINGS.

1/2 (16-ounce) package curly lasagna noodles (9 noodles)
2 cans (14 1/2 ounces each) stewed tomatoes
1 can (8 ounces) tomato sauce
1 container (15 ounces) part-skim ricotta cheese
2 ounces part-skim mozzarella cheese, shredded (1/2 cup)
3 tablespoons grated Parmesan cheese
4 tablespoons chopped fresh basil
1/2 teaspoon coarsely ground black pepper
2 teaspoons olive oil
1 small onion, chopped
1 small zucchini (4 ounces), finely chopped
1 small tomato, finely chopped
1 tablespoon capers, drained and chopped

1. In large saucepot, cook lasagna noodles as label directs. Drain and rinse with cold running water. Return noodles to saucepot with cold water to cover. Meanwhile, in 3-quart glass or ceramic baking dish, combine stewed tomatoes and tomato sauce; break up tomatoes with side of spoon.

2. Prepare filling: In large bowl, mix ricotta, mozzarella, Parmesan, 3 tablespoons basil, and pepper.

3. Preheat oven to 375°F. Place lasagna noodles on clean kitchen towels. Spread about 1/4 cup filling on each lasagna noodle and roll up jelly-roll fashion. Slice each rolled noodle crosswise in half. Arrange lasagna rolls, cut side down, in sauce in baking dish; cover loosely with foil. Bake until heated through, 35 to 40 minutes.

4. Meanwhile, prepare topping: In nonstick 10-inch skillet, heat oil over medium heat. Add onion; cook until tender and browned. Stir in zucchini; cook until tender. Stir in finely chopped tomato, capers, and remaining 1 tablespoon basil; heat through.

5. To serve, place sauce and lasagna rolls on 6 plates; spoon topping over lasagna rolls.

Each serving: About 335 calories (30 percent calories from fat), 18g protein, 42g carbohydrate, 11g total fat (6g saturated), 30mg cholesterol, 725mg sodium.

Linguine with Broccoli and Clams

Our lightened version of classic linguine with clam sauce includes healthy broccoli flowerets.

PREP: 30 MINUTES   COOK: 20 MINUTES   MAKES 4 MAIN-DISH SERVINGS.

salt

15 ounces broccoli flowerets (6 cups)

1 package (1 pound) linguine or spaghetti

1/2 cup dry white wine

2 dozen littleneck or small cherrystone clams, well scrubbed

1 tablespoon olive oil

2 garlic cloves, finely chopped

1/2 teaspoon coarsely ground black pepper

1/8 to 1/4 teaspoon crushed red pepper

1/4 cup loosely packed fresh parsley leaves, chopped

1. In large saucepot of boiling salted water, cook broccoli until almost tender, 4 to 6 minutes. With slotted spoon or metal strainer, transfer broccoli to bowl; do not discard cooking water. Rinse broccoli with cold running water to stop cooking.

2. In same saucepot of boiling water, cook pasta as label directs. Drain.

3. Meanwhile, in deep 12-inch skillet, heat wine to boiling over high heat. Add clams and reduce heat to medium. Cover and simmer until clams open, 7 to 10 minutes, transferring clams to large bowl as they open. Discard any clams that do not open. Strain clam broth through sieve lined with paper towels; add enough water to clam broth to equal 1 1/2 cups. When cool enough to handle, remove clams from shells and coarsely chop, adding any clam juices to reserved broth. (Reserve a few clams in the shell for garnish if you like.).

4. Clean skillet and wipe dry. Heat oil over medium heat. Add garlic and cook, stirring, 30 seconds. Add broccoli flowerets, black pepper, red pepper, clams, and reserved broth to skillet; cook, stirring gently, until heated through.

5. In warm serving bowl, toss hot pasta with broccoli mixture. Add reserved clams in shells and sprinkle with parsley.

Each serving: About 520 calories (10 percent calories from fat), 24g protein, 91g carbohydrate, 6g total fat (1g saturated), 18mg cholesterol, 360mg sodium.

Seafood Fra Diavolo

Shrimp and mussels adorn this festive pasta, while rings of tender squid provide extra flavor.

PREP: 25 MINUTES   COOK: 1 HOUR   MAKES 6 MAIN-DISH SERVINGS.

8 ounces cleaned squid
1 tablespoon olive oil
1 large garlic clove, finely chopped
1/4 teaspoon crushed red pepper
1 can (28 ounces) plum tomatoes
1/2 teaspoon salt
1 dozen mussels, scrubbed and debearded

8 ounces medium shrimp, shelled and deveined
1 package (16 ounces) linguine or spaghetti
1/4 cup chopped fresh parsley

1. Rinse squid and pat dry with paper towels. Slice squid bodies crosswise into 1/4-inch rings. Cut tentacles into several pieces if they are large.
2. In non-reactive 4-quart saucepan, heat oil over medium heat. Add garlic and crushed red pepper; cook just until fragrant, about 30 seconds. Stir in tomatoes with their juice and salt, breaking up tomatoes with side of spoon. Heat to boiling over high heat. Add squid and heat to boiling. Reduce heat; cover and simmer 30 minutes. Remove cover and simmer 15 minutes longer. Increase heat to high. Add mussels; cover and cook 3 minutes. Stir in shrimp; cover and cook until mussels open and shrimp are opaque throughout, about 2 minutes longer. Discard any mussels that do not open.
3. Meanwhile, in large saucepot, cook pasta as label directs. Drain. In warm serving bowl, toss pasta with seafood mixture and parsley.

Each serving: About 410 calories (11 percent calories from fat), 25g protein, 65g carbohydrate, 5g total fat (1g saturated), 140mg cholesterol, 588mg sodium.

Linguine with Scallops and Saffron

We flavored the creamy sauce with orange peel and saffron threads.

Prep: 20 minutes Cook: 15 minutes Makes 6 main-dish servings.

1 package (16 ounces) linguine or
  spaghetti
3 medium leeks (1 pound)
1 pound sea scallops, cut horizontally
  in half
2 tablespoons butter or margarine
3/4 teaspoon salt
1/4 teaspoon coarsely ground black
  pepper

1/2 teaspoon grated orange peel
large pinch saffron threads, crumbled
1/4 cup dry white wine
1 bottle (8 ounces) clam juice
1/4 cup heavy or whipping cream
1/2 cup loosely packed fresh parsley
  leaves

1. In large saucepot, cook pasta as label directs. Drain; return pasta to saucepot and keep warm.

2. Meanwhile, cut off root ends and tough green tops from leeks. Cut each leek lengthwise in half, then crosswise into 1/2-inch-wide slices. Place in large bowl of cold water. Use hands to swish leeks around to remove any grit or sand; repeat process, changing water several times. Drain well. Pull off and discard tough crescent-shaped muscle from each scallop.

3. In 12-inch skillet, melt margarine over medium heat. Add leeks, salt, and pepper; cook, stirring frequently, until leeks are soft, about 8 minutes. Add orange peel and saffron and cook, stirring, 2 minutes. Add wine; cook 1 minute longer. Increase heat to medium-high. Add clam juice and heat to boiling. Add scallops and cook until just opaque throughout, 3 to 4 minutes. Stir in cream and heat through.

4. Add leek mixture to pasta in saucepot; toss well. Sprinkle with parsley leaves just before serving.

Each serving: About 440 calories (18 percent calories from fat), 24g protein, 66g carbohydrate, 9g total fat (5g saturated), 50mg cholesterol, 622mg sodium.

Bow Ties with Shrimp and Fennel

The secrets to success here are a bag of frozen shrimp and a mixture of garlic and fennel seeds. If you don't have a mortar and pestle, crush garlic with a press and place the seeds in a sealed plastic bag, then mash with a rolling pin.

PREP: 10 MINUTES   COOK: 15 MINUTES   MAKES 6 MAIN-DISH SERVINGS.

1 package (16 ounces) bow-tie pasta
1 bag (16 ounces) frozen uncooked extra-large shrimp, shelled and deveined
1 cup frozen peas
1 small garlic clove
1 teaspoon fennel seeds
1/2 teaspoon salt

1/4 teaspoon coarsely ground black pepper
4 ripe medium tomatoes, finely chopped
2 tablespoons olive oil
2 ounces feta cheese, crumbled (1/2 cup)

1. In large saucepot, cook pasta as label directs. After pasta has cooked 12 minutes, add frozen shrimp and peas to pasta cooking water and continue cooking until pasta is done and shrimp turn opaque through-out, about 3 minutes. Drain pasta and shrimp; return to saucepot and keep warm.

2. Meanwhile, in mortar with pestle, crush garlic with fennel seeds, salt, and pepper. Transfer mixture to medium bowl and stir in tomatoes and olive oil.

3. Add tomato mixture and feta cheese to pasta and shrimp in saucepot; toss well.

Each serving: About 465 calories (17 percent calories from fat), 29g protein, 66g carbohydrate, 9g total fat (3g saturated), 125mg cholesterol, 520mg sodium.

Pad Thai

Pad Thai

Authentic Pad Thai is made with rice noodles (use the 1/8-inch-wide ones) that are available at Asian markets. If you can't find them, use angel hair pasta or linguine (cooked according to the package directions). It will still be delicious.

PREP: 25 MINUTES PLUS SOAKING NOODLES COOK: 5 MINUTES
MAKES 4 MAIN-DISH SERVINGS.

1 package (7 to 8 ounces) rice stick noodles (rice vermicelli), or 8 ounces angel hair pasta
1/4 cup fresh lime juice
1/4 cup Asian fish sauce (nam pla)
2 tablespoons sugar
1 tablespoon vegetable oil
8 ounces medium shrimp, shelled and deveined, then cut lengthwise in half
2 garlic cloves, finely chopped
1/4 teaspoon crushed red pepper
3 large eggs, lightly beaten
6 ounces bean sprouts (2 cups), rinsed and drained
1/3 cup unsalted roasted peanuts, coarsely chopped
3 green onions, thinly sliced
1/2 cup loosely packed fresh cilantro leaves
lime wedges

1. In large bowl, soak rice stick noodles, if using, in enough hot water to cover for 20 minutes. Drain. With kitchen shears, cut noodles into 4-inch lengths. If using angel hair pasta, break in half, cook in large saucepot as label directs, drain, and rinse with cold running water.

2. Meanwhile, in small bowl, combine lime juice, fish sauce, and sugar. Assemble all remaining ingredients and place next to stove.

3. In 12-inch skillet, heat oil over high heat until hot. Add shrimp, garlic, and crushed red pepper; cook, stirring, 1 minute. Add eggs and cook, stirring, until just set, about 20 seconds. Add drained noodles and cook, stirring, 2 minutes. Add fish-sauce mixture, half of bean sprouts, half of peanuts, and half of green onions; cook, stirring, 1 minute.

4. Transfer Pad Thai to warm platter or serving bowl. Top with remaining bean sprouts and sprinkle with remaining peanuts, remaining green onions, and cilantro. Serve with lime wedges.

Each serving: About 472 calories (30 percent calories from fat), 21g protein, 63g carbohydrate, 16g total fat (3g saturated), 230mg cholesterol, 811mg sodium.

Penne with Salmon and Asparagus

A white-wine-and-tarragon-infused broth is a luscious match to salmon in this ever-popular seafood-and-vegetable combination.

PREP: 15 MINUTES COOK: 30 MINUTES MAKES 6 MAIN-DISH SERVINGS.

1 package (16 ounces) penne rigate
   or bow-tie pasta
3 teaspoons olive oil
1 pound asparagus, trimmed and cut
   into 2-inch pieces
1/2 teaspoon salt
1/4 teaspoon coarsely ground black
   pepper

1 large shallot, finely chopped
   (1/4 cup)
1/3 cup dry white wine
1 cup low-sodium chicken broth
1 skinless salmon fillet (1 pound),
   cut crosswise into thirds, then
   lengthwise into 1/4-inch-thick slices
1 tablespoon chopped fresh tarragon

1. In large saucepot, cook pasta as label directs. Drain.

2. Meanwhile, in nonstick 12-inch skillet, heat 2 teaspoons oil over medium-high heat. Add asparagus, salt, and the pepper and cook until asparagus is almost tender-crisp, about 5 minutes. Add shallot and remaining 1 teaspoon oil; cook, stirring constantly, 2 minutes longer. Add wine; heat to boiling over high heat. Stir in broth and heat to boiling. Arrange salmon slices in skillet; cover and cook until just opaque throughout, 2 to 3 minutes. Remove skillet from heat; stir in tarragon. In warm serving bowl, toss pasta with asparagus mixture.

Each serving: About 470 calories (23 percent calories from fat), 27g protein, 60g carbohydrate, 12g total fat (2g saturated), 45mg cholesterol, 404mg sodium.

Sesame Noodles and Vegetables

If you have access to Asian ingredients, try this with fresh Chinese noodles. Cook the broccoli and carrots in the boiling water first, then add the fresh noodles for the last minute or so of cooking. They should cook in the time it takes the water to come back to boiling.

PREP: 10 MINUTES   COOK: 20 MINUTES   MAKES 6 MAIN-DISH SERVINGS.

1 package (16 ounces) linguine or spaghetti

1 package (7 to 8 ounces) broccoli flowerets

3 medium carrots, peeled and shredded

1 cup hot water

1/2 cup reduced-fat smooth peanut butter

3 tablespoons seasoned rice vinegar

3 tablespoons soy sauce

1 tablespoon Asian sesame oil

2 teaspoons sugar

2 ounces sliced cooked ham, cut into thin slivers

2 green onions, thinly sliced

1. In large saucepot, cook linguine as label directs, but do not add salt to water. After linguine has cooked 4 minutes, add broccoli and carrots to pasta cooking water. Continue cooking until the linguine is done and vegetables are tender-crisp, 5 to 10 minutes longer. Drain the linguine and vegetables; return to saucepot and keep warm.

2. Meanwhile, in medium bowl, combine hot water, peanut butter, rice vinegar, soy sauce, sesame oil, and sugar until smooth.

3. Add peanut sauce and ham to linguine mixture in saucepot; toss well. Spoon into large bowl; sprinkle with sliced green onions.

Each serving: About 490 calories (24 percent calories from fat), 19g protein, 76g carbohydrate, 13g total fat (2g saturated), 6mg cholesterol, 930mg sodium.

Spaghetti with Bacon and Peas

"The peas cook along with the pasta, and the sauce is really easy to make with ricotta and Romano cheese," says GH Food Director Susan Westmoreland of her speedy weeknight pasta dinner. Along with the spaghetti dish, she serves a side of sliced tomatoes, and fresh figs for dessert. To optimize the time it takes to prepare the meal, put water on to boil for the pasta, and while it heats, cook the bacon and onion. Then, as the pasta cooks, slice the tomatoes.

PREP: 10 MINUTES   COOK: 10 MINUTES   MAKES 6 MAIN-DISH SERVINGS.

1 pound thin spaghetti or vermicelli
1 package (10 ounces) frozen peas
4 slices bacon
1 medium onion, finely chopped
1 container (15 ounces) part-skim
  ricotta cheese

1/2 cup grated Pecorino Romano or
  Parmesan cheese
1/2 teaspoon salt
1/4 teaspoon coarsely ground black
  pepper

1. In large saucepot, cook pasta as label directs. During last 2 minutes of pasta cooking, add frozen peas to pasta cooking water; continue cooking until pasta is done. Drain, reserving 1 cup pasta cooking water. Return pasta and peas to saucepot and keep warm.

2. Meanwhile, in 12-inch skillet, cook bacon over medium heat until browned. Transfer to paper towels to drain. Pour off all but 1 tablespoon bacon drippings from skillet. Add onion and cook until tender and golden, 8 to 10 minutes.

3. Add reserved pasta water, onion mixture, ricotta, Romano, salt, and pepper to pasta and peas in saucepot. Crumble in bacon and toss again.

Each serving: About 497 calories (24 percent calories from fat), 25g protein, 69g carbohydrate, 13g total fat (7g saturated), 36mg cholesterol, 587mg sodium.

Spaghetti with
Bacon and Peas

Radiatori with Arugula, Cherry Tomatoes, and Pancetta

No need to cook the arugula in this easy dish; it quickly wilts when tossed with the hot pasta and sauce.

PREP: 15 MINUTES COOK: 10 MINUTES MAKES 4 MAIN-DISH SERVINGS.

1 package (16 ounces) radiatori or rotini pasta
4 ounces sliced pancetta or bacon, chopped
1 garlic clove, crushed with garlic press
1 pound cherry tomatoes, cut into quarters

$^1/_2$ teaspoon salt
$^1/_4$ teaspoon coarsely ground black pepper
2 bunches arugula (10 ounces each), trimmed
$^1/_4$ cup freshly grated Parmesan cheese

1. In large saucepot, cook pasta as label directs. Drain and keep warm.

2. Meanwhile, in nonstick 10-inch skillet, cook pancetta over medium heat until lightly browned. (If cooking bacon, discard all but 1 tablespoon bacon drippings.) Add garlic and cook, stirring, 30 seconds. Add tomatoes, salt, and pepper and cook until tomatoes are warmed through, 1 to 2 minutes longer.

3. In warm serving bowl, toss pasta with pancetta mixture, arugula, and Parmesan.

Each serving: About 557 calories (18 percent calories from fat), 22g protein, 93g carbohydrate, 11g total fat (4g saturated), 14mg cholesterol, 676mg sodium.

Nutrition Spotlight: Garlic

Garlic brings vivid flavor to lower-fat dishes, but its benefits extend far beyond taste. The latest research suggest that garlic is rich in plant chemicals that help lower "bad" (LDL) cholesterol.

Ziti with Sausage and Zucchini

Prep: 10 minutes   Cook: 15 minutes   Makes 6 main-dish servings.

1 package (16 ounces) ziti rigate or wagon-wheel pasta

12 ounces sweet Italian-sausage links, casings removed

3 medium zucchini (8 ounces each), each cut length-wise in half, then cut crosswise into 1/4-inch-thick slices

1/4 teaspoon salt

1/4 teaspoon coarsely ground black pepper

1 can (28 ounces) whole plum tomatoes

grated Parmesan cheese (optional)

1. In large saucepot, cook pasta as label directs. Drain; return pasta to saucepot and keep warm.

2. Meanwhile, heat nonstick 12-inch skillet over medium high heat. Add sausage meat and cook, stirring frequently to break up sausage, until browned, about 5 minutes. Transfer sausage to bowl.

3. Discard all but 1 tablespoon sausage drippings from skillet. Add zucchini, salt, and pepper and cook, stirring occasionally, until zucchini is golden, about 5 minutes. Stir in tomatoes with their juice; heat to boiling, breaking up tomatoes with side of spoon. Return sausage to skillet. Reduce heat to low; cover and simmer 5 minutes longer.

4. Add sausage mixture to pasta in saucepot; toss well. Serve with grated Parmesan cheese, if you like.

Each serving: About 475 calories (28 percent calories from fat), 21g protein, 66g carbohydrate, 15g total fat (5g saturated), 35mg cholesterol, 785mg sodium.

Spaghetti and Meatballs

A childhood favorite—with kids of all ages. We've baked the meatballs for leaner results. To further cut back on calories, reduce pasta portions.

PREP: 45 MINUTES   COOK: 45 MINUTES   MAKES 6 MAIN-DISH SERVINGS.

SPAGHETTI SAUCE
- 1 tablespoon olive oil
- 1 medium carrot, peeled and finely chopped
- 1 small onion, finely chopped
- 1 garlic clove, finely chopped
- 1 can (28 ounces) Italian-style tomatoes in puree
- 1 small bay leaf
- 1/4 teaspoon salt
- 1/8 teaspoon coarsely ground black pepper

MEATBALLS
- 2 slices firm white bread, diced
- 3 tablespoons water
- 1 pound lean ground beef or lean ground turkey
- 1 large egg white
- 2 tablespoons grated Pecorino Romano or Parmesan cheese
- 1 tablespoon grated onion
- 1 tablespoon finely chopped fresh parsley leaves
- 1 small garlic clove, crushed with garlic press
- 1/2 teaspoon salt
- 1 package (16 ounces) spaghetti, cooked as label directs

1. Prepare Spaghetti Sauce: In 3-quart saucepan, heat oil over medium heat. Add carrot and chopped onion and cook, stirring occasionally, until vegetables are very tender and golden, about 15 minutes. Add chopped garlic; cook, stirring, 1 minute.

2. Meanwhile, place tomatoes with their puree in bowl. With hands or slotted spoon, crush tomatoes well. Add tomatoes with their puree, bay leaf, salt and pepper to saucepan; heat to boiling over high heat. Reduce heat to low; cover and simmer 15 minutes. Uncover and simmer, stirring occasionally, 15 minutes longer. Discard bay leaf.

3. While sauce is cooking, prepare Meatballs: Preheat oven to 425°F. Line 13" by 9" metal baking pan with foil; spray foil with nonstick cooking spray.

4. In medium bowl, combine diced bread and water. With hand, mix until bread is evenly moistened. Add ground meat, egg white, Romano, grated onion, parsley, crushed garlic, and salt. With hand, mix until well combined.

5. Shape meat mixture into twelve 2-inch meatballs. (For easier shaping, use slightly wet hands.) Place meatballs in pan and bake until cooked through and lightly browned, 15 to 20 minutes. Add meatballs to sauce.
6. Place pasta in a large warm serving bowl; spoon meatballs and sauce over pasta.

Each serving: About 430 calories (17 percent calories from fat), 28g protein, 63g carbohydrate, 8g total fat (2g saturated), 144mg cholesterol, 520mg sodium.

Spaghetti and Meatballs

BEEF

Orange-Glazed Steak

We marinate round steak in a soy-and-garlic mixture, then brush it with orange marmalade for a tasty finish.

PREP: 5 MINUTES PLUS MARINATING GRILL: 25 MINUTES
MAKES 6 MAIN-DISH SERVINGS.

1/4 cup soy sauce
2 garlic cloves, crushed with garlic
  press
1 teaspoon coarsely ground black
  pepper

1 beef top round steak, 1 1/4 inches
  thick (2 pounds), well trimmed
1/3 cup orange marmalade

1. In 13" by 9" baking dish, combine soy sauce, garlic, and pepper. Add steak to soy-sauce mixture, turning to coat. Cover and refrigerate 30 minutes to marinate, turning once.

2. Prepare grill. Place steak on grill over medium heat and grill, brushing with orange marmalade during last 10 minutes of cooking and turning occasionally, 25 minutes for medium-rare or until desired doneness. Transfer steak to cutting board and let stand 10 minutes to set juices for easier slicing. Cut into thin slices across the grain.

Each serving: About 202 calories (18 percent calories from fat), 28g protein, 12g carbohydrate, 4g total fat (1g saturated), 72mg cholesterol, 419mg sodium.

Chunky Beef Stew

Lean beef, winter vegetables, and a richly flavored sauce make this a candidate for family suppers or casual entertaining.

PREP: 30 MINUTES   COOK: 1 HOUR   MAKES 6 MAIN-DISH SERVINGS.

1 pound lean beef for stew, trimmed and cut into 1-inch cubes
1 tablespoon vegetable oil
1/2 teaspoon salt
2 large stalks celery, chopped
1 large onion, chopped
1 can (14 1/2 ounces) stewed tomatoes
1 can (14 1/2 ounces) beef broth or 1 3/4 cups homemade
1 cup plus 2 tablespoons water
3 large potatoes (1 1/2 pounds), peeled and cut into 1 1/2-inch chunks

3 medium carrots (1/2 pound), peeled and cut into 3/4-inch chunks
3 medium turnips (3/4 pound), peeled and cut into 1 1/2-inch chunks
1 tablespoon soy sauce
1 teaspoon sugar
3/4 teaspoon browning and seasoning sauce (optional)
2 tablespoons all-purpose flour
1 package (10 ounces) frozen peas
2 tablespoons freshly grated lemon peel

1. Pat beef dry with paper towels. In 5-quart Dutch oven, heat vegetable oil over medium–high heat until very hot. Add beef, sprinkle with salt, and cook, turning pieces occasionally, until beef is browned on all sides. Transfer beef to bowl.

2. Add celery and onion to drippings in Dutch oven and cook, stirring, until lightly browned. Return beef to Dutch oven; stir in stewed tomatoes, broth, and 1 cup water. Heat to boiling over high heat. Reduce heat to low; cover and simmer 25 minutes.

3. Add potatoes, carrots, turnips, soy sauce, sugar, and the browning and seasoning sauce, if using; heat to boiling over high heat. Reduce heat to low; cover and simmer until meat and vegetables are fork-tender, about 20 minutes longer.

4. In cup, with fork, mix flour and remaining 2 tablespoons water until blended. Stir flour mixture into meat mixture; cook over medium–high heat until mixture boils and thickens slightly. Stir in frozen peas; heat through. Sprinkle with lemon peel.

Each serving: About 330 calories (19 percent calories from fat), 23g protein, 45g carbohydrate, 7g total fat (2g saturated), 53mg cholesterol, 905mg sodium.

Steak and Pepper Fajitas

Steak and Pepper Fajitas

Arrange the meat and condiments in pretty dishes and let everyone make his own.

PREP: 10 MINUTES   COOK: 20 MINUTES   MAKES 4 MAIN-DISH SERVINGS.

1 beef top round steak, 1 inch thick (3/4 pound), well trimmed
1 bottle (8 ounces) medium-hot chunky salsa
1 tablespoon light corn-oil spread (56% to 60% fat)
1 medium red onion, thinly sliced
1 medium green pepper, thinly sliced
1 medium red pepper, thinly sliced
2 tablespoons chopped fresh cilantro leaves

8 (6-inch) low-fat flour tortillas, warmed as label directs
1 container (8 ounces) fat-free sour cream
8 ounces fat-free sharp Cheddar cheese, shredded
chile peppers, lime wedges, and cilantro sprigs for garnish

1. Preheat broiler. Place steak on rack in broiling pan; spread 1/4 cup salsa on top. Place pan in broiler at closest position to source of heat; broil steak 8 minutes. Turn steak over and spread 1/4 cup salsa on top; broil 8 minutes longer for medium-rare or until desired doneness.

2. Meanwhile, in nonstick 12-inch skillet, melt corn-oil spread over medium-high heat. Add red onion, green pepper, and red pepper; cook until vegetables are tender-crisp. Stir in chopped cilantro. Spoon mixture into serving bowl.

3. To serve, place steak on cutting board; holding knife almost parallel to cutting surface, slice steak crosswise into thin slices. Serve sliced steak with pepper mixture, tortillas, sour cream, shredded cheese, and remaining salsa. Garnish with chile peppers, lime wedges, and cilantro.

Each serving: About 450 calories (14 percent calories from fat), 45g protein, 55g carbohydrate, 7g total fat (1g saturated), 51mg cholesterol, 1,060mg sodium.

Lean Beef Stroganoff

PREP: 20 MINUTES COOK: 30 MINUTES MAKES 6 MAIN-DISH SERVINGS.

1 boneless beef top sirloin steak, 3/4 inch thick (1 pound), well trimmed

3 teaspoons olive oil

1 pound medium mushrooms, trimmed and thickly sliced

1 medium onion, chopped

1 teaspoon cornstarch

1 cup beef broth

1/2 cup chili sauce

2 tablespoons spicy brown mustard

2 tablespoons plus 1/4 cup water

12 ounces sugar snap peas or snow peas, strings removed

2 bags (6 ounces each) radishes, halved if large

1/2 teaspoon salt

1 package (12 ounces) extra-wide curly noodles, cooked as label directs

6 tablespoons nonfat sour cream

2 tablespoons chopped fresh parsley leaves

1. Holding knife almost parallel to cutting surface, slice steak crosswise into very thin slices.

2. Spray nonstick 12-inch skillet lightly with olive oil nonstick cooking spray. Place skillet over medium-high heat and heat. Add half of meat and cook, stirring quickly and constantly, until meat loses its pink color, about 2 minutes. Transfer to bowl. Repeat with remaining meat but do not use nonstick spray again.

3. In same skillet, heat 2 teaspoons olive oil over medium-high heat. Add mushrooms and onion and cook, stirring, until tender. In cup, mix cornstarch and beef broth; stir into mushroom mixture with chili sauce and mustard. Cook, stirring, until mixture boils and thickens slightly. Return beef to skillet; heat through.

4. Meanwhile, in nonstick 10-inch skillet, heat remaining 1 teaspoon olive oil and 2 tablespoons water over medium-high heat until hot. Add sugar snap peas and cook until tender-crisp, 5 to 7 minutes. Transfer to bowl. In same skillet, cook radishes and remaining 1/4 cup water over medium-high heat, until tender-crisp, 5 to 7 minutes. Add sugar snap peas and salt to radishes; heat through.

5. Spoon noodles onto 6 dinner plates. Spoon beef mixture over noodles; top each serving with 1 tablespoon sour cream and sprinkle with parsley. Serve with sugar snap peas and radishes.

Each serving: About 430 calories (19 percent calories from fat), 30g protein, 58g carbohydrate, 9g total fat (2g saturated), 90mg cholesterol, 740mg sodium.

Orange Beef and Peppers

Prep: 20 minutes   Cook: 20 minutes   Makes 4 main-dish servings.

1 beef top round steak, 3/4 inch thick
   (1 pound), well trimmed
2 tablespoons soy sauce
3 large oranges
2 tablespoons butter or margarine
1 large red pepper, cut into
   1/4-inch-thick slices
1 large yellow pepper, cut into
   1/4-inch-thick slices

1 bunch green onions, cut into 2-inch
   pieces
1 1/2 teaspoons grated, peeled fresh
   ginger
3/4 teaspoon cornstarch
2 bunches arugula (8 ounces), stems
   trimmed

1. Cut steak lengthwise in half. Holding knife almost parallel to cutting surface, slice steak crosswise into 1/8-inch-thick slices. In bowl, toss steak with soy sauce.

2. With a sharp paring knife, cut peel and white pith from 2 oranges; cut the oranges crosswise into 1/4-inch-thick slices, then cut each slice in half. From remaining orange, grate 1 teaspoon peel and squeeze 1/2 cup juice.

3. In nonstick 12-inch skillet, melt 2 teaspoons margarine over medium-high heat. Add red pepper and yellow pepper and cook, stirring frequently, until tender-crisp; transfer to bowl.

4. In same skillet, melt 1 teaspoon margarine; add green onions and cook, stirring frequently, until tender-crisp; transfer to bowl with peppers.

5. In small bowl, mix grated orange peel, orange juice, ginger, and cornstarch until blended; set aside.

6. In same skillet, melt remaining 1 tablespoon margarine. Add half of beef mixture and cook, stirring quickly and constantly, just until beef loses its pink color; transfer to bowl with vegetables. In drippings in skillet, repeat with remaining beef mixture. Return vegetables and meat to skillet. Stir in orange-juice mixture and sliced oranges; cook until liquid boils and thickens slightly and mixture is heated through.

7. Serve beef mixture with arugula.

Each serving: About 270 calories (30 percent calories from fat), 29g protein, 19g carbohydrate, 9g total fat (5g saturated), 81mg cholesterol, 607mg sodium.

PORK

Cabbage-Wrapped Pork Roast

Pork and cabbage, a traditional pairing, is recast: the cabbage wrapping helps to keep today's leaner pork moist while it cooks.

PREP: 30 MINUTES ROAST: 1 HOUR MAKES 12 MAIN-DISH SERVINGS.

1 large head green cabbage
  (3 pounds)
1 bunch green onions
1 tablespoon finely chopped fresh
  thyme leaves or 1/2 teaspoon
  dried thyme
1/4 teaspoon ground black pepper
1 1/2 teaspoons salt
1 boneless pork loin roast
  (3 pounds), trimmed

1 cube or envelope chicken-flavor
  bouillon dissolved in 2 cups hot
  water
8 medium red potatoes
  (2 1/2 pounds)
1 tablespoon vegetable oil
1 teaspoon caraway seeds, crushed
1 pint cherry tomatoes
2 teaspoons cornstarch
2 tablespoons water

1. Remove 6 large outer leaves from cabbage; trim tough ribs from leaves. Reserve remaining cabbage. Cut off root ends of green onions.
2. In 5-quart Dutch oven or saucepot, heat 3 quarts water to boiling over high heat. Add cabbage leaves and cook, pressing leaves under water with tongs, until leaves are pliable, 3 to 5 minutes. With slotted spoon, transfer leaves to colander to drain. Add green onions to boiling water; blanch until just wilted, 10 seconds. Drain and pat dry with paper towels.
3. Preheat oven to 350°F. In cup, mix thyme, black pepper, and 1 teaspoon salt. Rub thyme mixture on pork roast. Wrap roast in wilted cabbage leaves; secure leaves with blanched green onions (you will probably have to tie 2 green onion leaves together so strand is long enough to wrap around the roast).
4. Place pork loin in 14" by 10" roasting pan. Pour bouillon mixture into pan. Roast pork, basting occasionally with pan juices, until meat thermometer inserted in center registers 155°F., about 1 hour (internal temperature will rise to about 160°F. upon standing).

Cabbage-Wrapped Pork Roast

5. Meanwhile, in 4-quart saucepan, heat potatoes and enough water to cover to boiling over high heat. Reduce heat to low; cover and simmer until potatoes are tender, about 20 minutes. Drain well and cut into 1/2-inch cubes.

6. Coarsely slice remaining cabbage. In nonstick 5-quart Dutch oven, heat oil over medium-high heat. Add cabbage, caraway seeds, and remaining 1/2 teaspoon salt; cook, stirring frequently, until cabbage is tender-crisp. Add potato cubes; heat through. Spoon cabbage mixture onto large warm platter.

7. In same Dutch oven, heat cherry tomatoes over medium-high heat until heated through.

8. When pork loin is done, place on platter with cabbage mixture. In cup, mix the cornstarch with water. Stir cornstarch mixture into drippings in roasting pan. Place roasting pan over high heat; heat to boiling and boil 1 minute. Skim fat from pan sauce. Spoon sauce over pork and cabbage and serve with cherry tomatoes.

Each serving: About 325 calories (30 percent calories from fat), 30g protein, 24g carbohydrate, 11g total fat (4g saturated), 50mg cholesterol, 435mg sodium.

Smoked Pork Chop Dinner

A fruit compote, such as Spicy Plum Compote (page 231), is the perfect dessert for this hearty German favorite.

PREP: 10 MINUTES   COOK: 1 HOUR   MAKES 4 MAIN-DISH SERVINGS.

4 smoked pork loin or rib chops, each 3/4 inch thick (7 ounces each), well trimmed

1 tablespoon vegetable oil

1 medium Granny Smith or Rome Beauty apple, cut in half and cored

1 bag (1 ounces) carrots, peeled and cut into bite-size chunks

1 1/2 pounds sauerkraut, rinsed and drained

1 can or bottle (12 ounces) beer or nonalcoholic beer

1/2 cup water

1/4 cup packed light or dark brown sugar

2 teaspoons caraway or fennel seeds, crushed

1. Pat pork chops dry with paper towels. In 12-inch skillet, heat oil over high heat until very hot. Add pork chops and cook until browned on both sides. Meanwhile, coarsely grate 1/2 of unpeeled apple.

2. To pork chops in skillet, add grated apple, carrots, sauerkraut, beer, water, brown sugar, and caraway seeds. Heat to boiling over high heat. Reduce heat to low; cover and simmer 35 minutes.

3. Cut remaining half apple into wedges; add to mixture in skillet. Cook, occasionally spooning liquid in skillet over pork chops, until carrots and pork chops are fork-tender, 10 minutes longer.

Each serving: About 380 calories (28 percent calories from fat), 32g protein, 36g carbohydrate, 12g total fat (3g saturated), 82mg cholesterol, 500mg sodium.

Brazilian Pork

Brazilian Pork

Serve these bold chops with a mixed green salad.

PREP: 15 MINUTES COOK: 15 MINUTES MAKES 4 MAIN-DISH SERVINGS.

4 boneless pork loin chops, 3/4 inch thick (5 ounces each), well trimmed
1/2 teaspoon ground cumin
1/2 teaspoon ground coriander
1/4 teaspoon dried thyme
1/8 teaspoon ground allspice
1/2 teaspoon salt
1 teaspoon olive oil
1 medium onion, chopped
3 garlic cloves, crushed with garlic press

1 can (15 to 19 ounces) black beans, rinsed and drained
1/2 cup chicken broth
1 tablespoon fresh lime juice
1/4 teaspoon coarsely ground black pepper
1/4 cup packed fresh cilantro, chopped
fresh orange wedges (optional)

1. Pat pork chops dry with paper towels. In cup, mix cumin, coriander, thyme, allspice, and 1/4 teaspoon salt. Rub spice mixture on pork chops.
2. Heat nonstick 12-inch skillet over medium-high heat until very hot. Add pork chops and cook 4 minutes; turn chops over and cook until lightly browned on the outside and still slightly pink on the inside, 3 to 4 minutes longer. Transfer pork to platter; cover with foil to keep warm.
3. In same skillet, heat oil over medium heat. Add onion and cook, stirring frequently, until golden, about 5 minutes. Add garlic and cook, stirring, 1 minute longer. Stir in beans, broth, lime juice, pepper, and remaining 1/4 teaspoon salt; heat through.
4. To serve, spoon bean mixture over pork; sprinkle with cilantro. Serve with orange wedges if you like.

Each serving: About 340 calories (29 percent calories from fat), 42g protein, 25g carbohydrate, 11g total fat (3g saturated), 76mg cholesterol, 760mg sodium.

Pork Tenderloin Cutlets with Plum Glaze

The cutlets and glaze can be prepped in advance—up to several hours ahead. The grilling takes only minutes.

PREP: 10 MINUTES   GRILL: 6 MINUTES   MAKES 4 MAIN-DISH SERVINGS.

1 pork tenderloin (1 pound), trimmed
3/4 teaspoon salt
1/4 teaspoon coarsely ground black pepper
1/2 cup plum jam or preserves
1 tablespoon brown sugar
1 tablespoon grated, peeled fresh ginger
2 garlic cloves, crushed with garlic press
1 tablespoon fresh lemon juice
1/2 teaspoon ground cinnamon
4 large plums (1 pound), each pitted and cut in half

1. Prepare grill. Using sharp knife, cut tenderloin lengthwise almost in half, being careful not to cut all the way through. Open and spread flat like a book. With meat mallet or between two sheets of plastic wrap or waxed paper with rolling pin, pound meat to 1/4-inch thickness. Cut crosswise into 4 equal pieces; sprinkle cutlets with salt and pepper.

2. In small bowl, combine plum jam, brown sugar, ginger, garlic, lemon juice, and cinnamon. Brush one side of each cutlet and cut side of each plum half with plum glaze. Place cutlets and plums on grill over medium heat, glaze side down, and grill 3 minutes. Brush cutlets and plums with remaining plum glaze; turn pork and plums over and grill until cutlets are lightly browned on both sides and just lose their pink color throughout and plums are hot, about 3 minutes longer.

Each serving: About 333 calories (16 percent calories from fat), 27g protein, 44g carbohydrate, 6g total fat (2g saturated), 80mg cholesterol, 509mg sodium.

Nutrition Spotlight: Plums

Colorful plums are an excellent source of vitamin C, plus they offer fiber and potassium. Try them split, pitted, and grilled; their natural sugars caramelize, boosting their sweetness without adding extra calories.

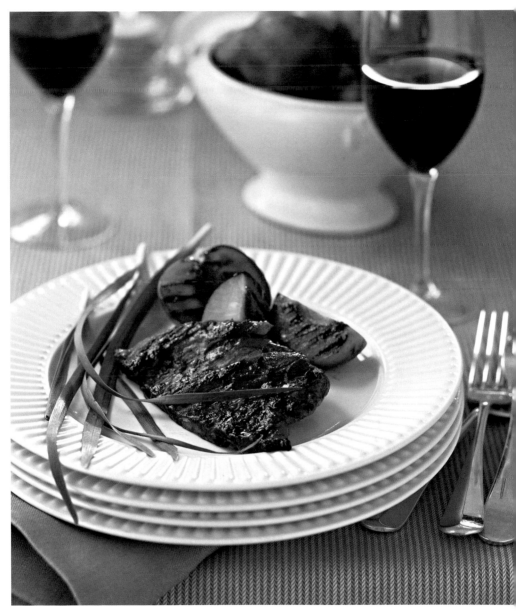

Pork Tenderloin Cutlets with Plum Glaze

Chinese-Style Pork and Baby Peas

Chinese-Style Pork and Baby Peas

Serve this one-skillet dinner with basmati rice—a long-grain variety that cooks in twenty minutes—for a well-rounded meal.

PREP: 10 MINUTES   COOK: 10 MINUTES
MAKES 4 MAIN-DISH SERVINGS.

2 teaspoons vegetable oil
1 pork tenderloin (1 pound), trimmed and cut into 1/4-inch-thick slices
2 garlic cloves, crushed with garlic press
1 package (10 ounces) frozen baby peas

3 tablespoons reduced-sodium soy sauce
2 tablespoons seasoned rice vinegar
1 tablespoon light (mild) molasses
1/4 teaspoon crushed red pepper

1. In nonstick 12-inch skillet, heat oil over medium-high heat. Add pork slices and garlic and cook, stirring occasionally, until pork slices are browned on the outside and just lose their pink color on the inside, about 6 minutes. Transfer pork to plate.

2. To same skillet, add peas, soy sauce, rice vinegar, ginger, molasses, and crushed red pepper; cook until peas are heated through, about 4 minutes. Return pork to skillet; toss to coat. To serve, spoon over rice.

Each serving: About 230 calories (23 percent calories from fat), 28g protein, 19g carbohydrate, 6g total fat (1g saturated), 64mg cholesterol, 840mg sodium.

What is Light Olive Oil?

"Light" refers to the oil's color and mild flavor, *not* its calorie count. (All olive oils are 100 percent fat and contain about 115 calories per tablespoon.) Light olive oil has a more neutral flavor than regular and extravirgin olive oil because it has gone through an extremely fine filtration process. It is a good choice for making baked goods and for sautéing or browning in recipes when you don't want the oil to flavor the dish.

Gingered Pork and Vegetable Stir-Fry

PREP: 15 MINUTES   COOK: 15 MINUTES   MAKES 4 MAIN-DISH SERVINGS.

1 pork tenderloin (12 ounces), thinly sliced
2 tablespoons grated, peeled fresh ginger
1 cup chicken broth
2 tablespoons teriyaki sauce
2 teaspoons cornstarch
2 teaspoons vegetable oil
8 ounces snow peas, strings removed
1 medium zucchini (8 ounces), halved lengthwise and thinly sliced
3 green onions, cut into 3-inch pieces

1. In medium bowl, toss pork and fresh ginger. In cup, mix broth, teriyaki sauce, and cornstarch.

2. In nonstick 12-inch skillet, heat 1 teaspoon oil over medium-high heat until hot. Add snow peas, zucchini, and green onions and cook, stirring frequently (stir-frying), until lightly browned and tender-crisp, about 5 minutes. Transfer to bowl.

3. In same skillet, heat remaining 1 teaspoon oil; add pork mixture and stir-fry until pork just loses its pink color. Transfer pork to bowl with vegetables. Stir cornstarch mixture; add to skillet and heat to boiling. Boil until sauce thickens, 1 minute. Stir in pork and vegetables; heat through.

Each serving: About 170 calories (26 percent calories from fat), 21g protein, 10g carbohydrate, 5g total fat (1g saturated), 51mg cholesterol, 550mg sodium.

Storing Fresh Gingerroot

To store fresh ginger, peel it and place in a screw-top jar. Pour enough vodka or dry sherry on top to completely cover the root, then seal the jar and refrigerate for up to one year. Grate or chop the gingerroot as needed.

POULTRY

Irish Chicken Dinner

Here's an interesting rendition of what New Englanders fondly call a boiled dinner, with chicken standing in for the traditional corned beef.

PREP: 20 MINUTES   COOK: 50 MINUTES   MAKES 4 MAIN-DISH SERVINGS.

1 chicken (3 1/2 pounds), cut into
   8 pieces and skin removed from all
   but wings
1 tablespoon vegetable oil
1 small head green cabbage
   (2 pounds), cut into 8 wedges
1 large onion, cut into 8 wedges
8 ounces carrots, peeled and cut into
   2 1/2-inch pieces

2 small turnips (8 ounces), peeled
   and cut into 1-inch-wide wedges
1 cup water
1 cup chicken broth
10 whole black peppercorns
3 whole cloves
1 large bay leaf
1 cup loosely packed spinach leaves,
   cut into 1/4-inch-wide strips

1. Cut each chicken breast half in half.

2. In 8-quart Dutch oven, heat oil over medium-high heat. Add cabbage and onion wedges and cook until lightly browned.

3. Add chicken, carrots, turnips, water, broth, peppercorns, cloves, and bay leaf to Dutch oven; heat to boiling over high heat. Reduce heat to low; cover and simmer, gently stirring occasionally, until chicken loses its pink color throughout and vegetables are tender, about 40 minutes.

4. With slotted spoon, transfer chicken and vegetables to 4 large soup bowls; top with spinach. Strain cooking broth through sieve into medium bowl; discard spices and bay leaf. Spoon hot broth over chicken and vegetables in soup bowls.

Each serving: About 380 calories (24 percent calories from fat), 46g protein, 27g carbohydrate, 10g total fat (2g saturated), 134mg cholesterol, 515mg sodium.

Thyme-Roasted Chicken and Vegetables

In just over an hour, you can have a one-dish meal of roasted chicken with fennel, potatoes, and onion ready to serve.

PREP: 20 MINUTES   ROAST: 50 MINUTES   MAKES 4 MAIN-DISH SERVINGS.

1 chicken (3 1/2 pounds), cut into
  8 pieces and skin removed from all
  but wings
1 pound all-purpose potatoes
  (3 medium), not peeled, cut into
  2-inch pieces
1 large fennel bulb (1 1/2 pounds),
  trimmed and cut into 8 wedges

1 large red onion, cut into 8 wedges
1 tablespoon chopped fresh thyme or
  1 teaspoon dried thyme
1 teaspoon salt
1/2 teaspoon ground black pepper
2 tablespoons olive oil
1/3 cup water

1. Preheat oven to 450°F. In large roasting pan (17" by 11 1/2"), arrange chicken pieces, skinned side up, and place potatoes, fennel, and onion around them. Sprinkle chicken with thyme, salt, and pepper. Drizzle oil over chicken and vegetables.

2. Roast chicken and vegetables 20 minutes; baste with drippings in pan. Roast, basting once more, until juices run clear when chicken breasts are pierced with tip of knife, about 20 minutes longer. Transfer chicken breasts to platter; keep warm.

3. Continue roasting remaining chicken pieces until juices run clear when thickest part of chicken is pierced with tip of knife and vegetables are fork-tender, about 10 minutes longer. Transfer chicken and vegetables to platter with breasts; keep warm.

4. Skim and discard fat from drippings in pan. To drippings, add water; heat to boiling over medium heat, stirring until brown bits are loosened from bottom. Spoon pan juices over chicken and vegetables.

Each serving: About 401 calories (29 percent calories from fat), 43g protein, 28g carbohydrate, 13g total fat (2g saturated), 124mg cholesterol, 870mg sodium.

Thyme-Roasted Chicken and Vegetables

Roasted Tandoori-Style Chicken Breasts

Plain yogurt tenderizes the chicken, while the exotic spices add plenty of flavor.

PREP: 10 MINUTES PLUS MARINATING   ROAST: 30 MINUTES
MAKES 6 MAIN-DISH SERVINGS.

2 limes
1 container (8 ounces) plain low-fat
  yogurt
1/2 small onion, chopped
1 tablespoon minced, peeled fresh
  ginger
1 tablespoon paprika
1 teaspoon ground cumin

1 teaspoon ground coriander
3/4 teaspoon salt
1/4 teaspoon ground red pepper
  (cayenne)
pinch ground cloves
6 medium bone-in chicken breast
  halves (3 pounds), skin removed

1. From 1 lime, squeeze 2 tablespoons juice. Cut remaining lime into 6 wedges; set aside for garnish. In blender, puree lime juice, yogurt, onion, ginger, paprika, cumin, coriander, salt, ground red pepper, and cloves until smooth. Place chicken and yogurt marinade in medium bowl or in ziptight plastic bag, turning to coat chicken. Cover bowl or seal bag and refrigerate chicken 30 minutes to marinate.

2. Preheat oven to 450°F. Arrange chicken on rack in medium roasting pan (14" by 10"). Spoon half of marinade over chicken; discard remaining marinade.

3. Roast chicken until juices run clear when thickest part of chicken is pierced with tip of knife, about 30 minutes.

4. Transfer chicken to warm platter; garnish with lime wedges to serve.

Each serving: About 197 calories (14 percent calories from fat), 36g protein, 5g carbohydrate, 3g total fat (1g saturated), 88mg cholesterol, 415mg sodium.

Sticky Drumsticks

Have lots of napkins on hand for these delicious oven-barbecued drumsticks guaranteed to be a favorite with the kids in your family.

PREP: 20 MINUTES BAKE: 35 MINUTES MAKES 6 MAIN-DISH SERVINGS.

1/2 cup apricot preserves
1/4 cup teriyaki sauce
1 tablespoon dark brown sugar
1 teaspoon cornstarch

1 teaspoon cider vinegar
1/4 teaspoon salt
12 medium chicken drumsticks
  (3 pounds), skin removed

1. Preheat oven to 425°F. In large bowl, with wire whisk, mix apricot preserves, teriyaki sauce, brown sugar, cornstarch, vinegar, and salt until blended. Add chicken, tossing to coat.

2. Spoon chicken and sauce into 15 1/2" by 10 1/2" jelly-roll pan. Bake 15 minutes. Remove chicken from oven; with pastry brush, brush chicken with sauce in pan. Continue baking, brushing with sauce every 5 minutes, until juices run clear when drumsticks are pierced with tip of knife, 15 to 20 minutes longer.

3. Remove chicken from oven; brush with sauce. Let chicken cool on jelly-roll pan 10 minutes. Transfer chicken to serving dish and spoon sauce over chicken.

Each serving: About 240 calories (15 percent calories from fat), 26g protein, 24g carbohydrate, 4g total fat (2g saturated), 96mg cholesterol, 660mg sodium.

The Skinny on Poultry

The breast is the most tender part of the bird—and also the leanest. A 3 1/2-ounce portion of breast meat without skin has about 4 grams of fat. The same amount of skinless dark meat has about 10 grams of fat. And keep in mind that removing poultry skin slashes the amount of fat almost in half. You may prefer, however, to cook poultry with the skin on to keep the moisture in. Then simply remove the skin before eating. The fat reduction is practically the same.

Baked "Fried" Chicken

Baked "Fried" Chicken

For this healthier version of fried chicken, skinless chicken pieces are dipped in a spicy bread-crumb coating and baked until crispy and golden brown. You won't miss the calories.

PREP: 15 MINUTES BAKE: 35 MINUTES MAKES 6 MAIN-DISH SERVINGS.

1/2 cup plain dried bread crumbs

1/4 cup freshly grated Parmesan cheese

2 tablespoons cornmeal

1/2 teaspoon ground red pepper (cayenne)

1 large egg white

1/2 teaspoon salt

1 chicken (3 1/2 pounds), cut into 8 pieces and skin removed from all but wings

1. Preheat oven to 425°F. Grease 15 1/2" by 10 1/2" jelly roll pan with olive oil nonstick cooking spray.

2. On waxed paper, combine bread crumbs, Parmesan, cornmeal, and ground red pepper. In pie plate, beat egg white and salt.

3. Dip each piece of chicken in egg-white mixture, then coat with crumb mixture, firmly pressing so mixture adheres. Arrange chicken in prepared pan; lightly coat chicken with cooking spray.

4. Bake chicken until coating is crisp and golden brown and juices run clear when thickest part of chicken is pierced with tip of knife, about 35 minutes.

Each serving: About 329 calories (25 percent calories from fat), 46g protein, 14g carbohydrate, 9g fat (3g saturated), 137mg cholesterol, 660mg sodium.

Chicken Breasts in Orange Sauce

Use sweet seedless oranges for this flavorful entrée.

PREP: 15 MINUTES   COOK: 30 MINUTES   MAKES 4 MAIN-DISH SERVINGS.

4 large navel oranges
4 medium bone-in chicken breast halves (2 1/2 pounds), skin removed
1/2 teaspoon salt
1/2 teaspoon coarsely ground black pepper
1/4 teaspoon dried thyme leaves

1 tablespoon olive oil
1/2 cup chicken broth
1/4 cup orange marmalade
1 teaspoon cornstarch

1. From 1 orange, with vegetable peeler, remove four 3-inch-long strips of peel (each about 3/4 inch wide). Cut peel lengthwise into very thin slivers. Squeeze enough juice from the peeled orange and 1 other orange to equal 2/3 cup. Cut peel and white pith from remaining 2 oranges. Cut each orange in half from stem to blossom end, then cut each half crosswise into 1/4-inch-thick slices; set aside.

2. Rub chicken breasts with salt, pepper, and thyme. In nonstick 12-inch skillet, heat oil over medium-high heat until very hot. Add chicken breasts and cook until golden brown, about 3 minutes per side. Add orange-peel slivers, orange juice, and broth; heat to boiling. Reduce heat to low; cover and simmer until juices run clear when thickest part of chicken is pierced with tip of knife, about 20 minutes. Transfer chicken to warm platter; keep warm.

3. In cup, mix orange marmalade and cornstarch until blended. Add marmalade mixture to skillet; heat to boiling. Cook, stirring constantly, until sauce thickens slightly, 1 minute. Stir in orange slices; heat through. Spoon sauce over chicken on platter.

Each serving: About 305 calories (18 percent calories from fat), 35g protein, 29g carbohydrate, 6g total fat (1g saturated), 82mg cholesterol, 460mg sodium.

Chicken Provençal

A melt-in-your-mouth stew flavored with orange peel and fennel seed.

PREP: 30 MINUTES   COOK: 1 HOUR   MAKES 8 MAIN-DISH SERVINGS.

2 teaspoons olive oil
2 pounds skinless, boneless chicken
  thighs, cut into quarters
3/4 teaspoon salt
2 medium red peppers, cut into
  1/4-inch-thick slices
1 medium yellow pepper, cut into
  1/4-inch-thick slices
1 jumbo onion (1 pound), thinly sliced

3 garlic cloves, crushed with garlic
  press
1 can (28 ounces) Italian-style plum
  tomatoes
1/4 teaspoon dried thyme leaves
1/4 teaspoon fennel seeds, crushed
3 strips (3" by 1" each) orange peel
1/2 cup loosely packed fresh basil
  leaves, chopped

1. In nonstick 5-quart Dutch oven, heat 1 teaspoon oil over medium-high heat until very hot. Add half of chicken and 1/4 teaspoon salt; cook, turning the pieces, until lightly browned on all sides, about 10 minutes. Transfer chicken to plate. Repeat with remaining oil, chicken, and 1/4 teaspoon salt.

2. To drippings in Dutch oven, add red peppers, yellow peppers, onion, and remaining 1/4 teaspoon salt; cook, stirring frequently, until vegetables are tender and lightly browned, about 20 minutes. Add garlic; cook 1 minute.

3. Return chicken to Dutch oven. Add tomatoes with their juice, thyme, fennel seeds, and orange peel, breaking up tomatoes with side of spoon; heat to boiling. Reduce heat to low; cover and simmer until chicken loses its pink color throughout, about 15 minutes. Sprinkle with basil to serve.

Each serving: About 200 calories (27 percent calories from fat), 25g protein, 13g carbohydrate, 6g total fat (1g saturated), 94mg cholesterol, 460mg sodium.

Baked Honey-Mustard Chicken and Vegetables

The beauty of this flavor-packed dinner? It all cooks in the oven at the same time.

PREP: 10 MINUTES BAKE: 50 MINUTES MAKES 4 MAIN-DISH SERVINGS.

1 1/2 pounds small red potatoes, quartered
1 jumbo onion (1 pound), cut into eighths
6 teaspoons olive oil
3/4 teaspoon salt

1/4 teaspoon coarsely ground black pepper
4 medium bone-in chicken breast halves (2 1/2 pounds), skin removed
2 tablespoons honey mustard

1. Preheat oven to 450°F. In 13" by 9" metal baking pan, toss potatoes and onion with 4 teaspoons oil, salt, and pepper. Place pan in oven on middle rack and bake 25 minutes.

2. Meanwhile, place chicken breasts in small roasting pan and coat with 1 teaspoon oil. In cup, mix remaining 1 teaspoon oil with honey mustard; set aside.

3. After vegetables have baked 25 minutes, remove pan from oven and carefully turn vegetables with metal spatula. Return vegetables to oven, placing pan on lower oven rack. Place chicken on upper rack. Bake 10 minutes.

4. Remove chicken from oven and brush with honey-mustard mixture. Return to oven and bake until juices run clear when thickest part of chicken is pierced with tip of knife and vegetables are golden, 12 to 15 minutes longer. Serve chicken with vegetables.

Each serving: About 380 calories (24 percent calories from fat), 31g protein, 44g carbohydrate, 10g total fat (1g saturated), 66mg cholesterol, 630mg sodium.

Baked Honey-Mustard Chicken and Vegetables

Country Captain Casserole

Country Captain Casserole

Though the exact origin of this well-known dish is often debated, its great flavor is never in dispute.

PREP: 30 MINUTES   BAKE: 1 HOUR   MAKES 8 MAIN-DISH SERVINGS.

2 tablespoons plus 1 teaspoon
  vegetable oil
2 chickens (3 1/2 pounds each), each
  cut into 8 pieces and skin removed
  from all but wings
2 medium onions, chopped
1 large Granny Smith apple, peeled,
  cored, and chopped
1 large green pepper, chopped
3 large garlic cloves, finely chopped
1 tablespoon grated, peeled fresh
  ginger

3 tablespoons curry powder
1/2 teaspoon coarsely ground black
  pepper
1/4 teaspoon ground cumin
1 can (28 ounces) plum tomatoes
  in puree
1 can (14 1/2 ounces) chicken broth
  or 1 3/4 cups homemade
1/2 cup dark seedless raisins
1 teaspoon salt
1/4 cup chopped fresh parsley

1. In nonreactive 8-quart Dutch oven, heat 2 tablespoons oil over medium-high heat until very hot. Add chicken, in batches, and cook until golden brown, about 5 minutes per side. Transfer chicken pieces to bowl as they are browned.

2. Preheat oven to 350°F. In same Dutch oven, heat remaining 1 teaspoon oil over medium-high heat. Add onions, apple, green pepper, garlic, and ginger; cook, stirring frequently, 2 minutes. Reduce heat to medium; cover and cook 5 minutes longer.

3. Stir in curry powder, black pepper, and cumin; cook 1 minute. Add tomatoes with their puree, broth, raisins, salt, and chicken pieces. Heat to boiling over high heat; boil 1 minute. Cover and place in oven. Bake 1 hour. Sprinkle with parsley.

Each serving: About 347 calories (29 percent calories from fat), 43g protein, 19g carbohydrate, 11g total fat (2g saturated), 133mg cholesterol, 825mg sodium.

Poulé au Pot with Tarragon

Stewed chicken and vegetables is a favorite Sunday supper in France. Use the leftover broth as the base for a soup.

PREP: 15 MINUTES   COOK: 1 HOUR   MAKES 4 MAIN-DISH SERVINGS.

3 medium leeks (1 pound)
1 chicken (3 1/2 pounds), cut into
  8 pieces
1 pound small red potatoes
1 bag (16 ounces) carrots, peeled
  and cut into 3-inch pieces
4 cups water

1 can (14 1/2 ounces) chicken broth
  or 1 3/4 cups homemade
1/2 teaspoon salt
1/4 teaspoon dried thyme
1/4 teaspoon ground black pepper
1 large sprig plus 1 tablespoon
  chopped fresh tarragon

1. Cut off roots and trim dark green tops from leeks; cut each leek lengthwise in half, then crosswise into 3-inch pieces. Rinse in large bowl of cold water, swishing to remove sand; transfer to colander to drain, leaving sand in bottom of bowl.

2. In 6- to 8-quart Dutch oven, combine leeks, chicken, potatoes, carrots, water, broth, salt, thyme, pepper, and tarragon sprig. Heat to boiling over high heat. Reduce heat; cover and simmer until chicken loses its pink color throughout, about 45 minutes.

3. With slotted spoon, transfer chicken and vegetables to serving bowl. Remove and discard skin from chicken. Skim and discard fat from broth. Pour 1 cup broth over chicken (refrigerate remaining broth for another use). To serve, sprinkle chopped tarragon on top.

Each serving: About 472 calories (21 percent calories from fat), 47g protein, 44g carbohydrate, 11g total fat (3g saturated), 127mg cholesterol, 859mg sodium.

Nutrition Spotlight: Allium Vegetables

Leeks, garlic, shallots, and onions have sulfur compounds that account for their distinctive flavor and aroma—and their nutritional benefits. They can inhibit the formation of blood clots and reduce the body's production of cholesterol. Studies suggest they may also defend against bacteria, fungi, viruses, and parasites, and reduce the risk of stomach cancer.

Arroz con Pollo

From Santiago to Miami to Madrid, different versions of this comforting chicken-and-rice dish are served almost everywhere Spanish is spoken.

PREP: 15 MINUTES   COOK: 40 MINUTES   MAKES 4 MAIN-DISH SERVINGS.

1 tablespoon vegetable oil
6 medium bone-in chicken thighs
  (1 1/2 pounds), skin and fat removed
1 medium onion, finely chopped
1 red pepper, chopped
1 garlic clove, finely chopped
1/8 teaspoon ground red pepper
  (cayenne)
1 cup regular long-grain rice
1 can (14 1/2 ounces) chicken broth
  or 1 3/4 cups homemade

1/4 cup water
1 strip (3" by 1/2") lemon peel
1/4 teaspoon dried oregano
1/4 teaspoon salt
1 cup frozen peas
1/4 cup chopped pimiento-stuffed
  olives (salad olives)
1/4 cup chopped fresh cilantro
lemon wedges

1. In 5-quart Dutch oven, heat oil over medium-high heat until very hot. Add chicken, in batches, and cook until golden brown, about 5 minutes per side. Transfer chicken pieces to bowl as they are browned.
2. Reduce heat to medium. Add onion and red pepper to Dutch oven and cook until tender, about 5 minutes. Stir in garlic and ground red pepper and cook 30 seconds. Add rice and cook, stirring, 1 minute. Stir in broth, water, lemon peel, oregano, salt, and chicken; heat to boiling. Reduce heat; cover and simmer until juices run clear when thickest part of chicken is pierced with tip of knife, about 20 minutes.
3. Stir in peas; cover and heat through. Remove from heat and let stand 5 minutes. Sprinkle with olives and cilantro; serve with lemon wedges.

Each serving: About 387 calories (21 percent calories from fat), 26g protein, 48g carbohydrate, 9g total fat (2g saturated), 81mg cholesterol, 927mg sodium.

Chicken and Sweet-Potato Stew

Coat chicken thighs with an exotic mix of cumin and cinnamon, then simmer with beta carotene–rich sweet potatoes in a creamy peanut-butter sauce. Delectable over brown rice.

PREP: 20 MINUTES   COOK: 45 MINUTES   MAKES 4 MAIN-DISH SERVINGS.

4 medium bone-in chicken thighs
  (1 1/2 pounds), skin removed
1 teaspoon ground cumin
1/4 teaspoon ground cinnamon
1 tablespoon olive oil
1 1/2 pounds sweet potatoes
  (3 medium), peeled and cut into
  1/2-inch chunks
1 medium onion, sliced

1 can (28 ounces) whole tomatoes
  in juice
3 tablespoons natural peanut butter
1/2 teaspoon salt
1/4 teaspoon crushed red pepper
2 garlic cloves, peeled
1/4 cup packed fresh cilantro leaves
  plus 2 tablespoons chopped
  cilantro leaves

1. Rub chicken thighs with cumin and cinnamon; set aside.

2. In nonstick 12-inch skillet, heat oil over medium heat. Add sweet potatoes and onion; cook, stirring occasionally, until onion is tender, 12 to 15 minutes. Transfer to plate.

3. Increase heat to medium-high. Add seasoned chicken to skillet and cook until lightly browned, about 3 minutes per side.

4. Meanwhile, drain tomatoes, reserving juice. Coarsely chop tomatoes and set aside. In blender at high speed or in food processor with knife blade attached, puree tomato juice, peanut butter, salt, crushed red pepper, garlic, and 1/4 cup cilantro leaves until smooth.

5. Add sweet-potato mixture, chopped tomatoes, and peanut-butter sauce to skillet with chicken; heat to boiling over high heat. Reduce heat to low; cover and simmer until chicken loses its pink color throughout, about 25 minutes. To serve, sprinkle with chopped cilantro.

Each serving: About 410 calories (26 percent calories from fat), 26g protein, 50g carbohydrate, 12g total fat (2g saturated), 76mg cholesterol, 725mg sodium.

Chicken Breasts with Six Quick Sauces

Simply sauté boneless chicken breasts, then take your pick from six easy sauces.

PREP: 2 MINUTES PLUS MAKING SAUCE COOK: 10 MINUTES
MAKES 4 MAIN-DISH SERVINGS.

1 teaspoon vegetable oil
4 small skinless, boneless chicken
  breast halves (1 pound)

choice of sauce (below)

1. In nonstick 12-inch skillet, heat oil over medium-high heat until very hot. Add chicken and cook until chicken is golden brown and loses its pink color throughout, 4 to 5 minutes per side. Transfer chicken to platter; keep warm.
2. Prepare sauce and serve.

Apple-Curry Sauce

After removing chicken, reduce heat to medium. Add 2 teaspoons vegetable oil to skillet. Add 1 Golden Delicious apple, peeled, cored, and chopped, and 1 small onion, chopped. Cook, stirring, until tender. Stir in 1 1/2 teaspoons curry powder and 1/4 teaspoon salt; cook 1 minute. Stir in 1/2 cup mango chutney, 1/2 cup frozen peas, and 1/2 cup water. Heat to boiling; boil 1 minute. Spoon over chicken.

Each serving with chicken: About 352 calories (13 percent calories from fat), 34g protein, 38g carbohydrate, 5g total fat (1g saturated), 82mg cholesterol, 596mg sodium.

Black Bean Salsa

After removing chicken, reduce heat to medium. Add 1 can (15 to 19 ounces) black beans, rinsed and drained, 1 jar (10 ounces) thick-and-chunky salsa, 1 can (8³/4 ounces) whole-kernel corn, drained, ¹/4 cup water, and 2 tablespoons chopped fresh cilantro to skillet. Cook, stirring, until heated through, about 1 minute. Spoon over chicken.

Each serving with chicken: About 282 calories (13 percent calories from fat), 38g protein, 22g carbohydrate, 4g total fat (1g saturated), 82mg cholesterol, 1,086mg sodium.

Chinese Ginger Sauce

After removing chicken, reduce heat to medium. Add 1 teaspoon vegetable oil to the skillet. Add 1 red pepper, thinly sliced, and cook until tender-crisp. Add ¹/2 cup water, 2 tablespoons soy sauce, 2 tablespoons seasoned rice vinegar, and 1 tablespoon grated, peeled fresh ginger. Heat to boiling; boil 1 minute. Spoon over chicken and sprinkle with 2 green onions, chopped.

Each serving with chicken: About 195 calories (18 percent calories from fat), 34g protein, 4g carbohydrate, 4g total fat (1g saturated), 82mg cholesterol, 757mg sodium.

Provençal Sauce

After removing chicken, reduce heat to medium. Add 1 teaspoon olive or vegetable oil to skillet. Add 1 medium onion, chopped, and cook, stirring, until tender. Stir in 1 can (14¹/2 ounces) Italian-style stewed tomatoes, ¹/2 cup pitted ripe olives, each cut in half, 1 tablespoon drained capers, and ¹/4 cup water. Cook, stirring, until heated through, about 1 minute. Spoon over chicken.

Each serving with chicken: About 253 calories (25 percent calories from fat), 35g protein, 11g carbohydrate, 7g total fat (1g saturated), 82mg cholesterol, 785mg sodium.

Creamy Mushroom Sauce

After removing chicken, add 1 teaspoon vegetable oil to skillet. Add 10 ounces mushrooms, trimmed and sliced, 1 medium onion, thinly sliced, and 3/4 teaspoon salt. Cook, stirring, until vegetables are golden brown and tender. Reduce heat to low; stir in 1/2 cup light sour cream and 1/4 cup water; heat through (do not boil). Spoon over chicken.

Each serving with chicken: About 260 calories (28 percent calories from fat), 37g protein, 9g carbohydrate, 8g total fat (3g saturated), 92mg cholesterol, 548mg sodium.

Dijon Sauce

After removing chicken, add 1/2 cup half-and-half or light cream, 2 table-spoons Dijon mustard with seeds, and 3/4 cup seedless red or green grapes, each cut in half, to skillet. Cook over low heat, stirring to blend flavors, until sauce has thickened, about 1 minute. Spoon over chicken.

Each serving with chicken: About 234 calories (27 percent calories from fat), 34g protein, 7g carbohydrate, 7g total fat (3g saturated), 93mg cholesterol, 285mg sodium.

Chicken-Breast Savvy

Companies now market several variations of this popular choice. For example, skinless, boneless breast halves may be labeled exactly that, or they may say skinless, boneless split breasts or portions. If the label doesn't indicate that the breast is cut into two pieces—the clues to look for are halves, split, or portions—it could be whole and would have to be halved.

Companies also package tenderloins (the narrow pieces of chicken from the underside of the breast). These could be labeled tenders or fillets—any which way, they're boneless, very tender, and perfect for chicken fingers, stir-fries, and salads. Thin-sliced chicken-breast cutlets are breast halves cut horizontally in half for quicker cooking (about 5 minutes), They're great in place of pounded chicken breasts, or instead of veal in veal scalloppine.

Balsamic Chicken and Pears

Balsamic vinegar has a unique sweet-and-sour flavor; use sparingly. Look for the word "tradizionale" on the label.

PREP: 10 MINUTES COOK: 20 MINUTES MAKES 4 MAIN-DISH SERVINGS.

2 teaspoons vegetable oil
4 small skinless, boneless chicken
  breast halves (1 pound)
2 Bosc pears, not peeled, each cut in
  half, cored, and cut into 8 wedges

1 cup chicken broth
3 tablespoons balsamic vinegar
2 teaspoons cornstarch
1 1/2 teaspoons sugar
1/4 cup dried cherries or raisins

1. In nonstick 12-inch skillet, heat 1 teaspoon oil over medium-high heat until very hot. Add chicken and cook until chicken is golden brown and loses its pink color throughout, 4 to 5 minutes per side. Transfer chicken to plate; keep warm.

2. In same skillet, heat remaining 1 teaspoon oil. Add pears and cook until tender and golden brown.

3. In cup, with fork, blend broth, vinegar, cornstarch, and sugar. Stir broth mixture and dried cherries into skillet with pears. Heat to boiling, stirring; boil 1 minute. Return chicken to skillet; heat through.

Each serving: About 235 calories (15 percent calories from fat), 27g protein, 22g carbohydrate, 4g total fat (1g saturated), 66mg cholesterol, 325mg sodium.

Balsamic Chicken and Pears

Chicken Breasts with Vegetable Ribbons

A quick sprinkle of lemon peel, garlic, and parsley adds a burst of flavor and an elegant touch.

PREP: 15 MINUTES COOK: 25 MINUTES MAKES 4 MAIN-DISH SERVINGS.

4 medium skinless, boneless chicken breast halves (1 1/4 pounds)
1/2 teaspoon salt
1/4 teaspoon coarsely ground black pepper
2 garlic cloves, finely chopped
2 teaspoons freshly grated lemon peel

1 tablespoon olive oil
3 medium carrots, peeled
2 medium zucchinis (1 pound)
3/4 cup chicken broth
1/2 cup water
1 cup loosely packed fresh parsley leaves, chopped

1. Sprinkle chicken with 1/4 teaspoon salt and the pepper. In cup, mix garlic, lemon peel, and remaining 1/4 teaspoon salt; set aside.

2. In nonstick 12-inch skillet, heat oil over medium-high heat until very hot. Add chicken and cook 6 minutes. Reduce heat to medium; turn chicken over and cook until chicken is golden brown and loses its pink color throughout, 6 to 8 minutes longer. Transfer chicken to platter; sprinkle with garlic mixture and keep warm.

3. Meanwhile, with sharp vegetable peeler, peel carrots lengthwise into wide, thin strips. Repeat with zucchini.

4. In same skillet, heat broth and water to boiling over high heat. Reduce heat to medium-low and add carrots; cover and cook 3 minutes. Add zucchini; cover and cook until vegetables are just tender, 5 to 7 minutes longer. Stir in all but 1 tablespoon parsley.

5. To serve, spoon vegetable ribbons and broth onto 4 dinner plates; top with chicken. Sprinkle with remaining parsley.

Each serving: About 240 calories (23 percent calories from fat), 36g protein, 10g carbohydrate, 6g total fat (1g saturated), 82mg cholesterol, 530mg sodium.

Skillet Lemon Chicken

Impressive enough to serve to guests. Steam up a bunch of fresh spring asparagus to serve alongside.

PREP: 15 MINUTES COOK: 10 MINUTES MAKES 4 MAIN-DISH SERVINGS.

4 medium skinless, boneless chicken breast halves (1 1/4 pounds)	1/2 cup fat-free chicken broth
1/2 teaspoon salt	1/4 cup dry white wine
2 teaspoons olive oil	2 tablespoons fresh lemon juice
3 garlic cloves, crushed with side of chef's knife	1 1/2 teaspoons all-purpose flour
	2 teaspoons butter or margarine
	1/2 lemon, thinly sliced

1. With meat mallet, or between 2 sheets of plastic wrap or waxed paper with rolling pin, pound chicken breast halves to 1/4-inch thickness. Sprinkle with salt.

2. In nonstick 12-inch skillet, heat oil over medium-high heat until very hot. Add chicken; cook 6 minutes. Reduce heat to medium; turn chicken over and cook until chicken is golden brown and loses its pink color throughout, 5 to 8 minutes longer. Transfer chicken to platter and keep warm.

3. Add garlic to skillet; cook until golden. In cup, with fork, mix broth, wine, lemon juice, and flour until smooth; stir into mixture in skillet and heat to boiling. Boil 1 minute. Stir in margarine. Discard garlic. Pour sauce over chicken and top with lemon slices.

Each serving: About 205 calories (26 percent calories from fat), 33g protein, 2g carbohydrate, 6g total fat (4g saturated), 98mg cholesterol, 462mg sodium.

Cooking with Wine

Wine adds fat-free flavor and body to quick pan sauces, stews, and poached fruit desserts. Because the success of the dish is determined by the quality of its ingredients, it is important to cook with good wine. Avoid the cooking wines sold in supermarkets; they're high in salt and low in flavor.

Chicken Cordon Bleu

Chicken Cordon Bleu

An elegant entrée made more healthful—and easier. Sautéed chicken breasts are topped with sliced ham and mozzarella and served on a bed of baby spinach.

PREP: 10 MINUTES   COOK: 15 MINUTES   MAKES 4 MAIN-DISH SERVINGS.

1 teaspoon butter or margarine
4 small skinless, boneless chicken
  breast halves (1 pound)
1/2 cup fat-free chicken broth
2 tablespoons balsamic vinegar
1/8 teaspoon coarsely ground black
  pepper

4 thin slices cooked ham (2 ounces)
4 thin slices part-skim mozzarella
  cheese (2 ounces)
1 bag (5 to 6 ounces) prewashed
  baby spinach

1. In nonstick 12-inch skillet, melt magarine over medium-high heat until hot. Add chicken and cook 5 minutes. Reduce heat to medium and turn chicken over; cover and cook until chicken is golden brown and just loses its pink color throughout, about 5 minutes longer.

2. Increase heat to medium-high. Stir in broth, vinegar, and pepper; cook, uncovered, 1 minute. Remove skillet from heat; top each chicken breast with a slice of ham, then a slice of cheese. Cover skillet until cheese melts, about 3 minutes.

3. Arrange spinach on large platter; top with chicken breasts and drizzle with pan sauce.

Each serving: About 210 calories (26 percent calories from fat), 34g protein, 5g carbohydrate, 6g total fat (4g saturated), 91mg cholesterol, 551mg sodium.

Jamaican Jerk Chicken Kabobs

Originally, jerk seasoning was only used to season pork shoulder, which was "jerked" apart into shreds before serving. Nowadays, this very popular power-packed seasoning rub is enjoyed on fish and chicken as well.

PREP: 15 MINUTES PLUS MARINATING BROIL: 10 MINUTES
MAKES 4 MAIN-DISH SERVINGS.

2 green onions, chopped
1 jalapeño chile, seeded and finely
  chopped
1 tablespoon minced, peeled fresh
  ginger
2 tablespoons white wine vinegar
2 tablespoons Worcestershire sauce
3 teaspoons vegetable oil

1 teaspoon ground allspice
1 teaspoon dried thyme
1/2 teaspoon plus 1/8 teaspoon salt
1 pound skinless, boneless chicken
  breast halves, cut into 12 pieces
1 red pepper, cut into 1-inch pieces
1 green pepper, cut into 1-inch pieces
4 metal skewers

1. In blender or in food processor with knife blade attached, process green onions, jalapeño, ginger, vinegar, Worcestershire, 2 teaspoons oil, allspice, thyme, and 1/2 teaspoon salt until paste forms.

2. Place chicken in small bowl or in ziptight plastic bag and add green-onion mixture, turning to coat chicken. Cover bowl or seal bag and refrigerate chicken 1 hour to marinate.

3. Meanwhile, in small bowl, toss red and green peppers with remaining 1 teaspoon oil and remaining 1/8 teaspoon salt.

4. Preheat broiler. Alternately thread chicken and pepper pieces onto skewers.

5. Place kabobs on rack in broiling pan. Brush kabobs with any remaining marinade. Place pan in broiler at closest position to heat source. Broil kabobs 5 minutes; turn and broil until chicken loses its pink color throughout, about 5 minutes longer.

Each serving: About 181 calories (25 percent calories from fat), 27g protein, 6g carbohydrate, 5g total fat (1g saturated), 66mg cholesterol, 525mg sodium.

Jamaican Jerk Chicken Kabobs

Thai Chicken with Basil

Thai Chicken with Basil

The essence of Thai cooking, the blending of cool and hot flavors, such as cilantro, basil, ginger, garlic, and chiles, lends an exotic touch to this stir-fry.

PREP: 20 MINUTES PLUS MARINATING COOK: 10 MINUTES
MAKES 4 MAIN-DISH SERVINGS.

1 pound skinless, boneless chicken breast halves
3 tablespoons Asian fish sauce (nuoc nam)
1 tablespoon soy sauce
1 tablespoon brown sugar
2 teaspoons vegetable oil
1 large onion (12 ounces), cut into 1/4-inch-thick slices

2 red or green chiles (serrano or jalapeño), seeded and cut into matchstick strips
2 teaspoons minced, peeled fresh ginger
2 garlic cloves, crushed with garlic press
1 1/2 cups loosely packed fresh basil leaves

1. Holding knife almost parallel to cutting surface, cut each chicken breast half crosswise into 1/4-inch-thick slices. In medium bowl, combine fish sauce, soy sauce, and brown sugar; add chicken slices, tossing to coat. Let marinate 5 minutes.

2. In nonstick 12-inch skillet, heat oil over medium-high heat until very hot. Add the chicken with marinade and cook, stirring frequently (stir-frying), until chicken loses its pink color throughout, 3 to 4 minutes. With slotted spoon, transfer chicken to bowl.

3. Add onion to marinade remaining in skillet and cook, stir-frying, until tender-crisp, about 4 minutes. Stir in chiles, ginger, and garlic; cook 1 minute longer.

4. Return chicken to skillet; heat through. Stir in basil leaves just before serving.

Each serving: About 238 calories (19 percent calories from fat), 3g protein, 16g carbohydrate, 5g total fat (1g saturated), 66mg cholesterol, 784mg sodium.

Grilled Chicken Breasts with Plum Salsa

Here's a quick dish that turns ordinary chicken into the specialty of the house. (The plum salsa can also be used to spice up plain fish and seafood dishes.)

PREP: 20 MINUTES PLUS MARINATING   GRILL: 10 MINUTES
MAKES 4 MAIN-DISH SERVINGS.

2 tablespoons seasoned rice vinegar

1/2 teaspoon salt

1/8 teaspoon coarsely ground black pepper

4 medium skinless, boneless chicken breast halves (1 1/4 pounds)

1 pound ripe purple and/or green plums (4 medium), chopped

1/4 cup finely chopped red onion

1/4 cup finely chopped yellow pepper

1/4 cup loosely packed fresh cilantro leaves, finely chopped

1 jalapeño chile, seeded and finely chopped

mixed baby greens (optional)

1. In pie plate, with wire whisk or fork, combine vinegar, salt, and black pepper. Spoon half of vinegar mixture into medium bowl. Add chicken breasts to mixture in pie plate, turning to coat. Cover and refrigerate 30 minutes to marinate, turning occasionally.

2. Meanwhile, prepare grill and spray grill rack (away from heat source) with nonstick cooking spray. Prepare the plum salsa: Stir plums, red onion, yellow pepper, cilantro, and jalapeño into vinegar mixture in bowl. Set plum salsa aside.

3. Place chicken breasts on grill over medium heat; discard marinade in pie plate. Grill chicken, turning once, until chicken loses its pink color throughout, 10 to 12 minutes. (If using a grill pan, spray pan with nonstick cooking spray and heat over medium heat until hot but not smoking. Add chicken breasts and cook, turning once, until chicken loses its pink color throughout, 10 to 12 minutes.)

4. To serve, place chicken on a bed of mixed baby greens if you like, and spoon plum salsa on top.

Each serving: About 245 calories (15 percent calories from fat), 36g protein, 14g carbohydrate, 4g total fat (1g saturated), 96mg cholesterol, 550mg sodium.

Grilled Chicken Breasts with Plum Salsa

Tortilla Chicken Tenders with Easy Corn Salsa

PREP: 15 MINUTES   BAKE: 10 MINUTES   MAKES 4 MAIN-DISH SERVINGS.

2 ounces baked tortilla chips
2 teaspoons chili powder
1/4 teaspoon salt
olive oil nonstick cooking spray
1 pound chicken tenders

2 ears corn, husks and silk removed
1 jar (11 to 12 ounces) mild salsa
1/4 cup loosely packed fresh cilantro leaves, chopped
lime wedges

1. Place tortilla chips in ziptight plastic bag. Crush chips with rolling pin to fine crumbs (you should have about 1/2 cup crumbs). On waxed paper, combine tortilla-chip crumbs, chili powder, and salt; set aside.

2. Preheat oven to 450°F. Spray 15 1/2" by 10 1/2" jelly-roll pan with olive oil spray. Place chicken tenders in medium bowl; spray with olive oil spray, tossing to coat well. Roll chicken in tortilla crumbs to coat; place in jelly-roll pan and spray again.

3. Bake chicken until it loses its pink color throughout, about 10 minutes.

4. Meanwhile, prepare corn salsa: Cut corn kernels from cobs; place in small bowl. Stir in salsa and cilantro until blended.

5. Serve chicken with corn salsa and lime wedges.

Each serving: About 245 calories (11 percent calories from fat), 30g protein, 24g carbohydrate, 3g total fat (0g saturated), 66mg cholesterol, 685mg sodium.

Chicken Breasts with Cumin, Coriander and Lime

An exotic blend of spices and lime juice adds instant flavor to boneless chicken breasts.

PREP: 10 MINUTES   COOK: 10 MINUTES   MAKES 4 MAIN-DISH SERVINGS.

3 tablespoons fresh lime juice (about 2 limes)
1 teaspoon ground cumin
1 teaspoon ground coriander
1 teaspoon sugar
1 teaspoon salt

1/8 teaspoon ground red pepper (cayenne)
4 small skinless, boneless chicken breast halves (1 pound)
1 tablespoon chopped fresh cilantro leaves

1. In large bowl, mix lime juice, cumin, coriander, sugar, salt, and ground red pepper; add chicken, tossing to coat.

2. Spray grill pan or cast-iron skillet with nonstick cooking spray; heat over medium-high heat until hot but not smoking. Add chicken and cook until chicken loses its pink color throughout, 5 to 6 minutes per side. Turn chicken once and brush with any remaining cumin mixture halfway through cooking. Place chicken breasts on platter; sprinkle with cilantro.

Each serving: About 150 calories (18 percent calories from fat), 27g protein, 3g carbohydrate, 3g total fat (1g saturated), 72mg cholesterol, 600mg sodium.

Grilled Chicken Breasts Saltimbocca

Grilled Chicken Breasts Saltimbocca

In Italian, saltimbocca means "jump in your mouth" and these irresistible prosciutto-and-sage-topped chicken breasts will do just that. One note of caution: Don't slice the prosciutto paper-thin, or it could burn.

PREP: 5 MINUTES GRILL: 10 MINUTES MAKES 4 MAIN-DISH SERVINGS.

4 medium skinless, boneless chicken breast halves (1 1/4 pounds)
1/8 teaspoon salt

1/8 teaspoon ground black pepper
12 fresh sage leaves
4 large slices prosciutto (4 ounces)

1. Prepare grill. Sprinkle chicken with salt and pepper. Place 3 sage leaves on each breast half. Place 1 prosciutto slice on top of each breast half, tucking in edges if necessary; secure with toothpicks.

2. Place chicken, prosciutto side down, on grill over medium heat and grill 5 to 6 minutes. Turn and grill until chicken loses its pink color throughout, 5 to 6 minutes longer.

Each serving: About 223 calories (24 percent calories from fat), 41g protein, 0g carbohydrate, 6g total fat (1g saturated), 105mg cholesterol, 690mg sodium.

TURKEY

Rosemary Roast Turkey Breast

When a whole turkey is too much, just use the breast.

PREP: 20 MINUTES ROAST: 2 HOURS 15 MINUTES
MAKES 10 MAIN-DISH SERVINGS.

1 bone-in turkey breast
  (6 to 7 pounds)
1 1/2 teaspoons dried rosemary,
  crumbled

1 teaspoon salt
3/4 teaspoon coarsely ground black
  pepper
1 cup chicken broth

1. Preheat oven to 350°F. Rinse turkey breast with cold running water and drain well; pat dry with paper towels. In cup, combine rosemary, salt, and pepper. Rub rosemary mixture all over turkey breast.

2. Place turkey, skin side up, on rack in small roasting pan (13" by 9"). Cover turkey with loose tent of foil.

3. Roast turkey 1 hour 30 minutes. Remove foil. Roast 45 to 60 minutes longer, occasionally basting with pan drippings. Start checking for doneness during last 30 minutes of cooking. Turkey breast is done when temperature on meat thermometer inserted into thickest part of breast (not touching bone) reaches 170°F. and juices run clear when thickest part of breast is pierced with tip of knife.

4. Transfer turkey to warm platter. Let stand 15 minutes to set juices for easier carving.

5. Meanwhile, pour broth into drippings in hot roasting pan. Heat to boiling over medium-high heat, stirring until browned bits are loosened from bottom of pan. Strain mixture through sieve into 1-quart saucepan; let stand 1 minute. Skim and discard fat. Heat pan-juice mixture over medium heat until hot; serve with turkey. Remove skin before eating.

Each serving without skin and with pan juices: About 251 calories (7 percent calories from fat), 55g protein, 0g carbohydrate, 2g total fat (0g saturated), 152mg cholesterol, 428mg sodium.

Turkey Meat Loaf

PREP: 20 MINUTES BAKE: 1 HOUR MAKES 8 MAIN-DISH SERVINGS.

1 tablespoon olive oil
2 medium stalks celery, finely chopped
1 small onion, finely chopped
2 garlic cloves, finely chopped
3/4 teaspoon ground cumin
1 1/2 pounds ground turkey breast
1/3 cup fresh bread crumbs

1/3 cup fat-free (skim) milk
1/3 cup bottled salsa
1 large egg white
1/2 teaspoon salt
1/2 teaspoon coarsely ground black pepper
1/4 cup ketchup
1 teaspoon Dijon mustard

1. In nonstick 10-inch skillet, heat oil over medium heat. Add celery and onion; cook, stirring often, until vegetables are tender, 10 minutes. Add garlic and cumin; cook, stirring, 30 seconds. Set vegetable mixture aside to cool slightly.

2. Preheat oven to 350°F. In large bowl, with hands, mix vegetable mixture, ground turkey, bread crumbs, milk, salsa, egg white, salt, and pepper until well combined but not overmixed.

3. In small bowl, mix ketchup and mustard; set aside.

4. In 13" by 9" metal baking pan, shape meat mixture into 9" by 5" loaf. Spread ketchup mixture over top of loaf. Bake meat loaf until meat thermometer inserted in center registers 160°F., about 1 hour (temperature will rise to 165°F. upon standing). Let meat loaf stand 10 minutes before removing from pan and slicing.

Each serving: About 145 calories (25 percent calories from fat), 20g protein, 5g carbohydrate, 4g total fat (1g saturated), 45mg cholesterol, 400mg sodium.

Turkey Chili

Turkey Chili

This spicy potful is made with lima beans and white beans—it's just right for a simple Sunday-evening supper. Serve with tortilla chips or corn bread.

PREP: 20 MINUTES   COOK: 20 MINUTES   MAKES 4 MAIN-DISH SERVINGS.

1 tablespoon olive oil
1 medium onion, chopped
3 garlic cloves, finely chopped
1 1/2 teaspoons chili powder
1 teaspoon ground cumin
1 teaspoon ground coriander
1/4 teaspoon salt
1/4 teaspoon coarsely ground black pepper
1 can (15 to 16 ounces) Great Northern or small white beans, rinsed and drained
1 can (14 1/2 ounces) reduced-sodium chicken broth or 1 3/4 cups homemade

1 package (10 ounces) frozen lima beans
1 can (4 to 4 1/2 ounces) chopped mild green chiles
8 ounces cooked turkey meat, cut into bite-size pieces (2 cups)
1 cup loosely packed fresh cilantro leaves, chopped
2 tablespoons fresh lime juice
lime wedges (optional)

1. In 5-quart Dutch oven, heat oil over medium heat. Add onion and cook, stirring often, until tender, about 5 minutes. Add garlic and cook 30 seconds. Stir in chili powder, cumin, coriander, salt, and pepper; cook 1 minute longer.

2. Meanwhile, in small bowl, mash half of the white beans.

3. Add mashed beans and unmashed beans, broth, frozen lima beans, green chiles, and turkey to Dutch oven. Heat to boiling over medium-high heat. Reduce heat to low; cover and simmer 5 minutes to blend flavors. Remove Dutch oven from heat; stir in cilantro and lime juice. Serve with lime wedges if you like.

Each serving: About 380 calories (19 percent calories from fat), 33g protein, 45g carbohydrate, 8g total fat (2g saturated), 44mg cholesterol, 995mg sodium.

Turkey Burgers and Coleslaw

Moist, juicy, and mildly spiced, these turkey burgers will satisfy any fast-food diehard. Paired with our sweet-and-tangy slaw, they make a great family dinner. Also great cold—for lunch-box sandwiches.

PREP: 15 MINUTES COOK: 20 MINUTES MAKES 4 MAIN-DISH SERVINGS.

BURGERS

1 teaspoon olive oil
1 small onion, finely chopped
1 garlic clove, crushed with garlic
 press
3 tablespoons water
1 pound ground turkey breast
1 large egg
1 slice firm white bread, crumbled
3 tablespoons mango chutney,
 chopped
1/2 teaspoon salt
1/4 teaspoon rubbed sage

COLESLAW

1 can (8 ounces) crushed pineapple
 in unsweetened juice
3 tablespoons chili sauce
1/2 teaspoon salt
1/8 teaspoon coarsely ground black
 pepper
1 bag (16 ounces) shredded cabbage
 mix for coleslaw

1. Prepare burgers: In nonstick 12-inch skillet, heat oil over medium heat. Add onion, garlic, and 1 tablespoon water and cook, stirring often, until onion is tender, 5 minutes. Transfer mixture to large bowl; set skillet aside.

2. Add remaining 2 tablespoons water, ground turkey, egg, bread, chutney, salt, and sage to onion mixture and mix well. With wet hands, shape mixture into four 1-inch-thick round patties.

3. Heat same skillet over medium heat until hot. Add patties and cook, turning once, until browned on both sides and cooked through, about 12 minutes.

4. Meanwhile, prepare coleslaw: In large bowl, stir pineapple with its juice, chili sauce, salt, and pepper until blended. Add cabbage mix and toss to coat. Serve burgers with coleslaw.

Each burger: About 210 calories (17 percent calories from fat), 28g protein, 13g carbohydrate, 4g total fat (1g saturated), 112mg cholesterol, 375mg sodium.

Each serving coleslaw: About 75 calories (0 calories from fat), 2g protein, 18g carbohydrate, 0g total fat, 0mg cholesterol, 460mg sodium.

Turkey Shepherd's Pies

Here's a good way to use up those Thanksgiving leftovers: A turkey-meat filling is topped with leftover mashed potatoes. Although the canned chicken broth called for here works well, we recommend using the turkey carcass to make a flavorful homemade turkey broth.

PREP: 30 MINUTES BAKE: 30 MINUTES MAKES 4 MAIN-DISH SERVINGS.

1 tablespoon olive oil
2 medium carrots, finely chopped
1 medium onion, finely chopped
1 medium celery stalk, finely
  chopped
2 cups mashed potatoes
3/4 cup milk
2 tablespoons all-purpose flour

1 cup chicken broth or turkey broth
8 ounces cooked turkey meat, cut
  into bite-size pieces (2 cups)
1 cup frozen peas
1/4 teaspoon salt
1/8 teaspoon coarsely ground black
  pepper
pinch dried thyme

1. In 5- to 6-quart Dutch oven, heat oil over medium heat. Add carrots, onion, and celery; cook until vegetables are tender and lightly browned, about 15 minutes.

2. Meanwhile, in small bowl, stir mashed potatoes with 1/4 cup milk until combined.

3. Preheat oven to 450°F. In cup, with fork, mix flour with broth and remaining 1/2 cup milk until blended. Pour broth mixture into Dutch oven with vegetables. Cook over high heat, stirring often, until mixture boils and thickens slightly. Boil 1 minute. Reduce heat to medium; add turkey, frozen peas, salt, pepper, and thyme; heat through.

4. Place four 11/2-cup ramekins or soufflé dishes on 151/2" by 101/2" jelly-roll pan for easier handling. Spoon warm turkey mixture into ramekins; top with potato mixture. Bake until hot and bubbly and potatoes are lightly browned, 30 minutes.

Each serving: About 320 calories (28 percent calories from fat), 25g protein, 33g carbohydrate, 10g total fat (3g saturated), 54mg cholesterol, 615mg sodium.

SEAFOOD

Moules à la Marinière

This is the way French cooks like to serve mussels. Use a crisp white wine, such as sauvignon blanc, or a dry vermouth, which adds extra flavor because of the herbs used in the distillation process.

PREP: 20 MINUTES COOK: 15 MINUTES MAKES 4 MAIN-DISH SERVINGS.

1 1/2 cups dry white wine or dry vermouth

1/3 cup finely chopped shallots or red onion

2 garlic cloves, finely chopped

1 tablespoon butter or olive oil

1/2 teaspoon salt

pinch ground black pepper

4 pounds mussels, preferably cultivated, scrubbed and debearded

1/4 cup chopped fresh parsley

1. In nonreactive 5-quart Dutch oven, combine wine, shallots, garlic, butter, salt, and pepper; heat to boiling over high heat. Boil 2 minutes.

2. Add mussels; heat to boiling. Reduce heat; cover and simmer until mussels open, about 5 minutes, transferring mussels to large bowl as they open. Discard any mussels that do not open. Pour mussel broth over mussels and sprinkle with parsley.

Each serving: About 212 calories (25 percent calories from fat), 16g protein, 9g carbohydrate, 6g total fat (2g saturated), 45mg cholesterol, 703mg sodium.

Crab Boil

A big pot of spiced boiled crabs, a Chesapeake Bay tradition, is a delicious but messy affair. Cover the table with newspaper and have lots of large napkins on hand. Serve with coleslaw and rolls. (If you want to cook crab so you can use the meat for another recipe, omit the crab boil seasoning and red pepper.)

PREP: 5 MINUTES COOK: 40 MINUTES MAKES 4 MAIN-DISH SERVINGS.

2 medium onions, coarsely chopped
1 carrot, peeled and coarsely
   chopped
1 stalk celery, coarsely chopped
1 lemon, sliced
1/2 cup crab boil seasoning

1 tablespoon crushed red pepper
1 tablespoon salt
1 gallon (16 cups) water
1 can or bottle (12 ounces) beer
2 dozen live hard-shell blue crabs,
   rinsed

1. In 12-quart stockpot, combine onions, carrot, celery, lemon, crab boil seasoning, crushed red pepper, salt, water, and beer. Heat to boiling over high heat; cook 15 minutes.

2. Using tongs, transfer crabs to stockpot. Cover and heat to boiling. Boil 5 minutes (crabs will turn red). With tongs, transfer crabs to colander to drain, then place on platter.

3. To eat crab, twist off claws and legs, then crack shell to remove meat. Break off flat pointed apron from underside of crab; remove top shell. Discard feathery gills. With kitchen shears or hands, break body in half down center. With fingers or lobster pick, remove meat.

Each serving: About 123 calories (15 percent calories from fat), 24g protein, 0g carbohydrate, 2g total fat (0g saturated), 119mg cholesterol, 1,410mg sodium.

Pan-Seared Scallops with Lemon Couscous

PREP: 20 MINUTES   COOK: 25 MINUTES   MAKES 6 MAIN-DISH SERVINGS.

4 teaspoons vegetable oil
1 large red pepper, thinly sliced
1 medium onion, thinly sliced
12 ounces medium mushrooms,
  trimmed and quartered
1 3/4 cups water
8 ounces sugar snap peas, strings
  removed

1 medium lemon
1 cup couscous (Moroccan pasta)
3/4 teaspoon salt
1 pound sea scallops
2 tablespoons soy sauce
2 bunches arugula (8 ounces), stems
  trimmed

1. In nonstick 12-inch skillet, heat 2 teaspoons oil over medium–high heat until hot. Add red pepper and onion and cook, stirring occasionally, until golden brown. Transfer red-pepper mixture to plate. In same skillet, heat 1 teaspoon oil; add mushrooms and cook until golden brown. Transfer mushrooms to plate with red-pepper mixture. Add 1/4 cup water to same skillet; heat to boiling. Add sugar snap peas and cook until tender-crisp, 3 to 4 minutes. Drain and set aside.

2. Meanwhile, from lemon, grate 1/2 teaspoon peel and squeeze 1 1/2 teaspoons juice. In 2-quart saucepan, heat lemon juice and remaining 1 1/2 cups water to boiling over high heat. Stir in couscous and salt. Cover saucepan and remove from heat. Let stand 5 minutes; stir in lemon peel. Keep warm.

3. Pull off and discard tough crescent-shaped muscle from each scallop. Pat scallops dry with paper towels. Wipe skillet dry and heat remaining 1 teaspoon oil over medium–high heat until hot. Add scallops and cook, turning once, until lightly browned on the outside and just opaque throughout, 3 to 4 minutes.

4. Return mushroom-pepper mixture to skillet; stir in soy sauce. Cook mixture over medium–high heat until heated through. Stir in sugar snap peas. Arrange arugula on plates. Top with couscous and scallop mixture.

Each serving: About 263 calories (14 percent calories from fat), 20g protein, 36g carbohydrate, 4g total fat (1g saturated), 25mg cholesterol, 770mg sodium.

Shrimp Curry and Rice

This tastes as good as classic slow-cooking curry, but is ready in a flash.

PREP: 10 MINUTES COOK: 20 MINUTES MAKES 4 MAIN-DISH SERVINGS.

1 cup regular long-grain rice
2 teaspoons olive oil
1 medium onion, finely chopped
1 tablespoon curry powder
1 teaspoon mustard seeds
1 pound large shrimp, shelled and
  deveined, leaving tail part of shell
  on, if you like

1/2 cup light coconut milk (not
  cream of coconut)
3/4 cup frozen peas, thawed
1 cup frozen whole baby carrots,
  thawed
1/2 teaspoon salt
chopped fresh cilantro leaves
  (optional)

1. Prepare rice as label directs but do not add margarine or butter.
2. Meanwhile, in nonstick 12-inch skillet, heat 1 teaspoon oil over medium-high heat. Reduce heat to medium; add onion and cook until tender, 8 minutes. Add curry powder and cook, stirring, 1 minute. Transfer onion mixture to medium bowl.
3. Increase heat to medium-high. In same skillet, heat remaining 1 teaspoon oil. Add mustard seeds; cook, stirring, 30 seconds. Add shrimp and cook, stirring frequently, until opaque throughout, 4 minutes.
4. Return onion mixture to skillet; stir in coconut milk, peas, carrots, and salt; heat through. Serve over rice. Sprinkle with cilantro if you like.

Each serving: About 390 calories (18 percent calories from fat), 30g protein, 49g carbohydrate, 8g total fat (2g saturated), 175mg cholesterol, 490mg sodium.

Frozen Shrimp

Flavorful shrimp, with just under two grams of fat in a four-ounce serving, is a savvy dieter's favorite seafood. And even better: Frozen shrimp is a bargain! The shrimp is either individually frozen and sold in bags or (more often) sold in blocks. Put the individually frozen shrimp in a colander and place under cold running water until thawed. For block-frozen shrimp, place under cold running water, and pull off the amount of shrimp you need as they thaw; return the remaining block of shrimp to the freezer.

Jamaican Jerk Snapper with Grilled Pineapple

Other fish fillets like sole and flounder would also work well with these zesty flavors.

PREP: 15 MINUTES   GRILL: 10 MINUTES   MAKES 4 MAIN-DISH SERVINGS.

2 green onions, chopped
1 jalapeño chile, seeded and chopped
2 tablespoons white wine vinegar
2 tablespoons Worcestershire sauce
1 tablespoon minced, peeled fresh ginger
1 tablespoon vegetable oil
1 1/4 teaspoons dried thyme

1 teaspoon ground allspice
1/4 teaspoon salt
4 red snapper fillets (5 ounces each)
1 small pineapple, cut lengthwise into 4 wedges or crosswise into 1/2-inch-thick slices
2 tablespoons brown sugar

1. Prepare grill. In medium bowl, mix green onions, jalapeño chile, vinegar, Worcestershire, ginger, oil, thyme, allspice, and salt until combined. Add snapper fillets to bowl, turning to coat; let stand 5 minutes.

2. Meanwhile, rub pineapple wedges or slices with brown sugar.

3. Place pineapple and snapper on grill over medium heat. Spoon half of jerk mixture remaining in bowl on snapper. Grill pineapple and snapper 5 minutes, then turn over. Spoon remaining jerk mixture on fish and grill until fish is just opaque throughout and pineapple is golden brown, 5 to 7 minutes longer.

Each serving: About 280 calories (26 percent calories from fat), 24g protein, 25g carbohydrate, 8g total fat (1g saturated), 52mg cholesterol, 305mg sodium.

Jamaican Jerk Snapper with Grilled Pineapple

Shrimp and Scallop Kabobs

One word of advice: Don't let the shellfish sit in the soy and rice vinegar mixture for more than a minute or two. The vinegar will firm and "cook" the flesh.

PREP: 20 MINUTES GRILL: 6 MINUTES MAKES 6 MAIN-DISH SERVINGS.

12 ounces large sea scallops
1 pound large shrimp, shelled and deveined, leaving tail part of shell on, if you like
3 tablespoons soy sauce
3 tablespoons seasoned rice vinegar
1 tablespoon Asian sesame oil
2 tablespoons grated, peeled fresh ginger

2 garlic cloves, crushed with garlic press
1 tablespoon brown sugar
1 bunch green onions, cut on diagonal into 3-inch pieces
12 cherry tomatoes
6 long metal skewers

1. Prepare grill. Pull off and discard tough crescent-shaped muscle from each scallop. Pat shrimp and scallops dry with paper towels.

2. In large bowl, combine soy sauce, vinegar, sesame oil, ginger, garlic, and brown sugar. Add shrimp and scallops, tossing to coat.

3. Alternately thread shrimp, scallops, green-onion pieces, and cherry tomatoes onto skewers. Place skewers on grill over medium heat and grill, turning skewers occasionally and brushing shrimp and scallops with any remaining soy-sauce mixture during first half of cooking, until shrimp and scallops are just opaque throughout, 6 to 8 minutes.

Each serving: About 168 calories (21 percent calories from fat), 23g protein, 9g carbohydrate, 4g total fat (1g saturated), 112mg cholesterol, 851mg sodium.

Grilled Thai Snapper Packets

Grilling snapper fillets in foil packets keeps the meat intact, and Thai seasonings give the fish a distinctive Asian flavor.

PREP: 25 MINUTES GRILL: 8 MINUTES MAKES 4 MAIN-DISH SERVINGS.

3 tablespoons fresh lime juice
1 tablespoon Asian fish sauce
  (nuoc nam)
1 tablespoon olive oil
1 teaspoon grated, peeled fresh
  ginger
1 small garlic clove, finely chopped

1/2 teaspoon sugar
4 red snapper fillets (6 ounces each)
1 large carrot, peeled and cut into
  2 1/4" by 1/4" matchstick strips
1 large green onion, thinly sliced
1/4 cup tightly packed fresh cilantro

1. Prepare grill. In small bowl, with wire whisk, whisk lime juice, fish sauce, oil, ginger, garlic, and sugar. With tweezers, remove any bones from snapper fillets.

2. From roll of foil, cut four 16" by 12" sheets. Fold each sheet crosswise in half, then open up like a book.

3. Place 1 snapper fillet, skin side down, on one half of each piece of foil. Evenly sprinkle fillets with carrot, green onion, and cilantro; drizzle with lime-juice mixture. Fold unfilled half of foil over fish. To seal, fold and crimp edges of foil all around.

4. Place packets on grill over medium heat; grill 8 minutes. To serve, cut packets open.

Each serving: About 228 calories (24 percent calories from fat), 36g protein, 5g carbohydrate, 6g total fat (1g saturated), 63mg cholesterol, 268mg sodium.

Another Good Reason to Eat Fish

Despite a reputation for clogging arteries and packing on unwanted pounds, all fats are not villainous. Indeed, one type of polyunsaturated fat, omega-3, is thought to combat heart disease. Omega-3s help inhibit the formation of blood clots and reduce the incidence of heartbeat abnormalities. You'll find omega-3s in fish—and the oilier the fish (like salmon, mackerel, and sardines) the more omega-3 it contains.

Grilled Tuna with Tuscan White Beans

Serve fresh tuna steak slices on a bed of warm cannellini beans seasoned with lemon, garlic, and sage. With two cans of beans, a pound of tuna stretches nicely to six servings.

PREP: 35 MINUTES   GRILL/BROIL: 4 MINUTES
MAKES 6 MAIN-DISH SERVINGS.

1 lemon
1 tablespoon plus 3 teaspoons
   extravirgin olive oil
1 medium onion, chopped
1 medium stalk celery, finely chopped
2 garlic cloves, crushed with garlic
   press
6 large fresh sage leaves, thinly sliced
2 cans (15 to 19 ounces each) white
   kidney beans (cannellini), rinsed
   and drained

1 teaspoon salt
1/2 teaspoon coarsely ground black
   pepper
1 tuna steak, 1 inch thick (1 pound),
   cut into 1/2-inch-thick slices
2 medium plum tomatoes, finely
   chopped
1 tablespoon chopped fresh parsley
   leaves for garnish

1. From lemon, grate 1/2 teaspoon peel and squeeze 2 tablespoons juice.
2. In 3-quart saucepan, heat 1 tablespoon plus 1 teaspoon oil over medium heat. Add onion and celery; cook, stirring occasionally, until tender, about 12 minutes. Add garlic, sage, and lemon peel; cook, stirring, 1 minute. Add beans, lemon juice, 1/2 teaspoon salt, and 1/4 teaspoon pepper; cook, stirring gently, until heated through.
3. Meanwhile, brush both sides of tuna with remaining 2 teaspoons oil and sprinkle with remaining 1/2 teaspoon salt and 1/4 teaspoon pepper.
4. Heat grill pan over medium-high heat until hot. Add tuna and cook, turning once, until just opaque throughout, 3 to 4 minutes. (Or, preheat broiler. Place tuna on rack in broiling pan; place pan in broiler at closest position to heat source; broil tuna 3 to 4 minutes.)
5. Place warm bean mixture on platter and top with tuna. Sprinkle with diced tomatoes and chopped parsley.

Each serving: About 275 calories (20 percent calories from fat), 27g protein, 30g carbohydrate, 6g total fat (1g saturated), 33mg cholesterol, 745mg sodium.

Lentils and Cod

The fennel and orange in this recipe bring home the flavors of Provence.

PREP: 40 MINUTES BAKE: 25 MINUTES MAKES 6 MAIN-DISH SERVINGS.

8 ounces lentils (1 cup)
1 tablespoon olive oil
2 medium carrots, finely chopped
1 medium onion, finely chopped
1 large stalk celery, finely chopped
1/2 teaspoon herbes de Provence*
1/4 teaspoon fennel seeds
3 strips (3" by 1" each) orange peel
3 garlic cloves, crushed with garlic
   press

2 cups water
1 can (14 1/2 ounces) reduced-
   sodium chicken broth or 1 3/4 cups
   homemade
1 can (14 1/2 ounces) tomatoes in
   puree
3/4 teaspoon salt
1/2 teaspoon coarsely ground black
   pepper
4 pieces cod fillet (6 ounces each)

1. Preheat oven to 400°F. Rinse lentils with cold running water and discard any stones or shriveled lentils. Set aside.

2. In 4-quart saucepan, heat oil over medium-high heat. Add carrots, onion, and celery; cook, stirring occasionally, until lightly browned, about 10 minutes. Add herbes de Provence, fennel seeds, orange peel, and garlic; cook, stirring, 2 minutes.

3. Add lentils, water, and broth; heat to boiling over high heat. Reduce heat to low; cover and simmer, stirring occasionally, 20 minutes. Add tomatoes with their puree, 1/2 teaspoon salt, and 1/4 teaspoon pepper, stirring and breaking up tomatoes with side of spoon. Heat to boiling over high heat. Reduce heat to low; cover and simmer 5 minutes longer.

4. Transfer lentil mixture to shallow 2 1/2-quart casserole. Place cod fillets on top of lentil mixture; sprinkle cod with remaining 1/4 teaspoon salt and 1/4 teaspoon pepper. Cover and bake until fish is just opaque throughout and lentil mixture is heated through, 20 to 25 minutes. Discard orange peel.

Each serving: About 325 calories (11 percent calories from fat), 32g protein, 40g carbohydrate, 4g total fat (1g saturated), 49mg cholesterol, 760mg sodium.

* If you can't find herbes de Provence, substitute 1/4 teaspoon each dried thyme and rosemary, crushed, and increase fennel seeds to 1/2 teaspoon.

Baked Scrod with Fennel and Potatoes

Baked Scrod with Fennel and Potatoes

A simple dish that only needs a green salad to become a complete meal.

PREP: 15 MINUTES BAKE: 55 MINUTES MAKES 4 MAIN-DISH SERVINGS.

1 1/2 pounds red potatoes (4 large), thinly sliced
1 medium fennel bulb (1 pound), trimmed and thinly sliced, feathery tops reserved
1 garlic clove, finely chopped
2 tablespoons olive oil

3/4 plus 1/8 teaspoon salt
1/2 teaspoon coarsely ground black pepper
4 pieces scrod fillet (5 ounces each)
1 large ripe tomato (8 ounces), seeded and chopped

1. Preheat oven to 425°F. In shallow 2 1/2-quart baking dish, toss potatoes, fennel, garlic, oil, 3/4 teaspoon salt, and 1/4 teaspoon pepper until well combined; spread evenly in baking dish. Bake, stirring once, until vegetables are tender and lightly browned, about 45 minutes.

2. With tweezers, remove any bones from scrod. Sprinkle scrod with remaining 1/8 teaspoon salt and remaining 1/4 teaspoon pepper. Arrange on top of potato mixture. Bake until fish is just opaque throughout, 10 to 15 minutes. Sprinkle with tomato and garnish with reserved fennel tops.

Each serving: About 335 calories (21 percent calories from fat), 30g protein, 35g carbohydrate, 8g total fat (1g saturated), 61mg cholesterol, 679mg sodium.

Fennel

Both fennel and anise are herbs of the carrot family, but anise has a sweeter, stronger licoricelike flavor. Fennel is cultivated for its bulb foliage, and its seeds. Look for pearly white fennel bulbs with no cracks or browning; you want them to be heavy for their size. The stalks should still be attached and have pale-green leaves.

Miso-Glazed Salmon

Brian Hagiwara, one of *Good Housekeeping*'s favorite food photographers, shared this special recipe. We love the taste of the rich salmon with the sweet and savory glaze. Serve with a side of steamed rice.

PREP: 10 MINUTES   BROIL: 10 MINUTES   MAKES 4 MAIN-DISH SERVINGS.

1/4 cup white miso
5 teaspoons sugar
4 teaspoons seasoned rice vinegar
1 tablespoon water
2 teaspoons minced, peeled fresh
  ginger

4 salmon steaks, 1 inch thick
  (6 ounces each)
1 green onion, thinly sliced diagonally

1. Preheat broiler. Lightly spray rack in broiling pan with nonstick cooking spray.

2. In small bowl, mix miso, sugar, vinegar, water, and ginger; set aside.

3. Place salmon steaks on rack in broiling pan. Place pan in broiler at closest position to heat source; broil salmon 5 minutes. Remove pan from broiler and spread half of miso mixture on salmon; broil 1 minute longer.

4. Remove pan from broiler; turn salmon over and top with remaining miso mixture. Broil salmon until miso mixture is bubbly and salmon is opaque throughout, 3 to 4 minutes longer. Sprinkle with green onion before serving.

Each serving: About 260 calories (24 percent calories from fat), 35g protein, 13g carbohydrate, 7g total fat (1g saturated), 86mg cholesterol, 870mg sodium.

Miso-Glazed Salmon

Mustard-Dill Salmon with Herbed Potatoes

A light and creamy sauce adds piquant flavor to succulent salmon. After you make the sauce, sauté snow peas in a nonstick skillet with a teaspoon of vegetable oil for a healthy side dish.

PREP: 20 MINUTES   BROIL: 8 MINUTES   MAKES 4 MAIN-DISH SERVINGS.

12 ounces small red potatoes, cut into 1-inch chunks
12 ounces small white potatoes, cut into 1-inch chunks
1 1/2 teaspoons salt
3 tablespoons chopped fresh dill
1/2 teaspoon coarsely ground black pepper

4 pieces salmon fillet (6 ounces each)
2 tablespoons light mayonnaise
1 tablespoon white wine vinegar
2 teaspoons Dijon mustard
3/4 teaspoon sugar

1. In 3-quart saucepan, heat potatoes, 1 teaspoon salt, and enough water to cover to boiling over high heat. Reduce heat to low; cover and simmer until potatoes are fork-tender, about 15 minutes. Drain potatoes and toss with 1 tablespoon dill, 1/4 teaspoon salt, and 1/4 teaspoon coarsely ground black pepper; keep the potatoes warm.

2. Meanwhile, preheat broiler. Grease rack in broiling pan. Place salmon on rack; sprinkle with 1/8 teaspoon salt and 1/8 teaspoon coarsely ground black pepper. Place broiling pan at closest position to heat source. Broil until salmon is just opaque throughout, 8 to 10 minutes.

3. While salmon is broiling, prepare sauce: In small bowl, mix mayonnaise, vinegar, mustard, sugar, remaining 2 tablespoons dill, 1/8 teaspoon salt, and 1/8 teaspoon black pepper.

4. Serve salmon with sauce and potatoes.

Each serving: About 335 calories (19 percent calories from fat), 37g protein, 31g carbohydrate, 7g total fat (1g saturated), 86mg cholesterol, 655mg sodium.

Curried Vegetable Stew

Serve over brown rice for a healthful vegetarian meal.

PREP: 15 MINUTES   COOK: 25 MINUTES   MAKES 4 MAIN-DISH SERVINGS.

2 teaspoons olive oil
1 large sweet potato (12 ounces),
  peeled and cut into 1/2-inch pieces
1 medium onion, cut into 1/2-inch
  pieces
1 medium zucchini (8 ounces), cut
  into 1-inch pieces
1 small green pepper, cut into
  3/4-inch pieces

1 1/2 teaspoons curry powder
1 teaspoon ground cumin
1 can (15 to 19 ounces) garbanzo
  beans, rinsed and drained
1 can (14 1/2 ounces) diced
  tomatoes
3/4 cup vegetable broth
1/2 teaspoon salt

1. In deep nonstick 12-inch skillet, heat oil over medium–high heat. Add sweet potato, onion, zucchini, and green pepper; cook, stirring, until vegetables are tender, 8 to 10 minutes. Add curry powder and cumin; cook 1 minute.

2. Add garbanzo beans, tomatoes with their juice, broth, and salt; heat to boiling over high heat. Reduce heat to medium–low; cover and simmer until vegetables are very tender but still hold their shape, about 10 minutes longer.

Each serving: About 223 calories (20 percent calories from fat), 8g protein, 39g carbohydrate, 5g total fat (0g saturated), 0mg cholesterol, 790mg sodium.

Easy Barbecued Beans and Rice

Easy Barbecued Beans and Rice

This vegetarian skillet dinner is especially good with a rich, smoky barbecue sauce.

PREP: 15 MINUTES COOK: 25 MINUTES MAKES 6 MAIN-DISH SERVINGS.

3/4 cup regular long-grain rice
1 tablespoon vegetable oil
1 medium green pepper, cut into
  1/2-inch pieces
1 medium red pepper, cut into
  1/2-inch pieces
1 medium onion, chopped
1 can (15 to 19 ounces) black beans,
  rinsed and drained
1 can (15 to 19 ounces) red kidney
  beans, rinsed and drained

1 can (15 to 19 ounces) garbanzo
  beans, rinsed and drained
1 can (15 to 16 ounces) pink beans,
  rinsed and drained
1 can (14 1/2 ounces) no-salt-added
  stewed tomatoes
1 cup water
1/2 cup bottled barbecue sauce

1. In 2-quart saucepan, prepare rice as label directs but do not add butter or margarine.

2. Meanwhile, in 12-inch skillet, heat oil over medium heat until hot. Add peppers and onion and cook, stirring, until tender. Add black beans, red kidney beans, garbanzo beans, pink beans, stewed tomatoes, water, and barbecue sauce; heat to boiling over high heat. Reduce heat to low; cover and simmer 15 minutes.

3. Spoon rice into center of beans. Before serving, stir to combine rice and bean mixture.

Each serving: About 355 calories (13 percent calories from fat), 16g protein, 61g carbohydrate, 5g total fat (1g saturated), 0mg cholesterol, 790mg sodium.

Winter Vegetable Chili

Serve this black-bean chili with a stack of warmed tortillas.

PREP: 15 MINUTES   COOK: 1 HOUR 15 MINUTES
MAKES 6 MAIN-DISH SERVINGS.

4 teaspoons olive oil
1 medium butternut squash
  (1 3/4 pounds), peeled and cut
  into 3/4-inch pieces
2 carrots, peeled and chopped
1 medium onion, chopped
3 tablespoons chili powder
1 can (28 ounces) plum tomatoes

1 can (4 to 4 1/2 ounces) chopped
  mild green chiles
1 cup vegetable broth
1/4 teaspoon salt
2 cans (15 to 19 ounces each) black
  beans, rinsed and drained
1/4 cup chopped fresh cilantro
sour cream or yogurt (optional)

1. In nonreactive 5-quart Dutch oven, heat 2 teaspoons oil over medium-high heat. Add squash; cook until golden. Transfer to bowl.

2. In same Dutch oven, heat remaining 2 teaspoons oil. Add carrots and onion; cook, stirring occasionally, until well browned. Stir in chili powder; cook, stirring, 1 minute. Add tomatoes with their juice, chiles with their liquid, broth, and salt. Heat to boiling over high heat, breaking up tomatoes with side of spoon. Reduce heat; cover and simmer 30 minutes.

3. Stir in beans and squash; heat to boiling over high heat. Reduce heat; cover and simmer until squash is tender and chili has thickened, about 15 minutes. Stir in cilantro. Serve with sour cream, if you like.

Each serving: About 233 calories (19 percent calories from fat), 9g protein, 42g carbohydrate, 5g total fat (1g saturated), 0mg cholesterol, 911mg sodium.

Nutrition Spotlight: Winter Squash

Take your pick of acorn, banana, butternut, delicate, and Hubbard squash, all at about 50 calories per half cup. Like its pumpkin cousin, squash is rich in the antioxidant beta-carotene, though the amount varies with the color of the flesh. For the biggest nutritional punch, go with deep yellow and orange flesh varieties.

Skillet Vegetable Curry

A package of precut cauliflower shortens prep time. As vegetables simmer, toast some pita bread to serve alongside.

PREP: 15 MINUTES   COOK: 20 MINUTES

MAKES ABOUT 4 MAIN-DISH SERVINGS.

12 ounces cauliflower flowerets

1 large all-purpose potato (8 ounces), peeled and cut into 1-inch chunks

1 large sweet potato (12 ounces), peeled and cut into 1-inch chunks

2 tablespoons lightly packed flaked sweetened coconut

2 teaspoons olive oil

1 medium onion, finely chopped

1 teaspoon mustard seeds

1 1/2 teaspoons ground cumin

1 1/2 teaspoons ground coriander

1/8 teaspoon ground red pepper (cayenne)

2 medium tomatoes, finely chopped

1 cup frozen peas, thawed

1 1/4 teaspoons salt

1/2 cup loosely packed fresh cilantro leaves, chopped

1. In 4-quart saucepan, heat cauliflower, potato, sweet potato, and enough water to cover to boiling over high heat. Reduce heat to low; cover and simmer until vegetables are tender, 8 to 10 minutes. Drain well, reserving 3/4 cup cooking water.

2. Meanwhile, in nonstick 12-inch skillet, cook coconut over medium heat, stirring constantly, until lightly browned, about 3 minutes; transfer to small bowl.

3. In same skillet, heat oil over medium heat; add onion and cook 5 minutes. Add mustard seeds, cumin, coriander, and ground red pepper; cover and cook, shaking skillet frequently, until onion is tender and lightly browned and seeds start to pop, 5 minutes longer.

4. Spoon cauliflower mixture into skillet; add reserved cooking water, toasted coconut, tomatoes, peas, and salt; heat through. Sprinkle with cilantro to serve.

Each serving: About 230 calories (16 percent calories from fat), 8g protein, 43g carbohydrate, 4g total fat (1g saturated), 0mg cholesterol, 735mg sodium.

Vegetable Omelet

More vegetables and fewer whole eggs make this a great healthy choice.

PREP: 30 MINUTES   BAKE/BROIL: 12 MINUTES
MAKES 4 MAIN-DISH SERVINGS.

8 ounces red potatoes, cut into
  1/2-inch pieces
1 medium onion, finely chopped
1 medium red pepper, cut into
  1/2-inch pieces
1 medium green pepper, cut into
  1/2-inch pieces
1 small zucchini (8 ounces), cut into
  1/2-inch pieces
1 teaspoon sugar

3/4 teaspoon salt
1/4 teaspoon coarsely ground black
  pepper
1/4 cup water
4 tablespoons chopped fresh basil
  leaves
6 large egg whites
2 large eggs
1/2 cup crumbled feta cheese
  (2 ounces)

1. In small saucepan, heat potatoes and enough water to cover to boiling over high heat. Reduce heat to low; cover and simmer until tender, about 10 minutes. Drain.

2. Spray nonstick 12-inch skillet with nonstick cooking spray. Add onion and cook over medium–high heat until golden. Add red pepper, green pepper, zucchini, sugar, salt, and black pepper and cook, stirring frequently, until vegetables are tender-crisp. Stir in water and heat to boiling. Reduce heat to low; cover and simmer until vegetables are tender, 10 minutes. Remove skillet from heat; stir in potatoes and 1 tablespoon basil.

3. Preheat oven to 375°F. In medium bowl, with wire whisk or fork, mix egg whites, eggs, 1/4 cup crumbled feta, and remaining 3 tablespoons basil.

4. Spray oven-safe 10-inch skillet with nonstick cooking spray. (Wrap handle of skillet with double layer of foil if handle is not oven-safe.) Pour egg mixture into pan and cook over medium–high heat until egg mixture begins to set, 1 to 2 minutes. Remove skillet from heat. With slotted spoon, spread vegetable mixture over egg mixture in skillet; sprinkle with remaining 1/4 cup crumbled feta. Bake omelet until set, 10 minutes. If you like, broil 1 to 2 minutes to brown top of omelet.

Each serving: About 185 calories (29 percent calories from fat), 13g protein, 20g carbohydrate, 6g total fat (3g saturated), 119mg cholesterol, 860mg sodium.

California Frittata

Mexican-style salsa, crisp jicama, and tortillas contribute as much to the California flavor of this robust frittata as does the medley of fresh vegetables. An egg substitute may be used instead of the eggs.

PREP: 30 MINUTES   COOK: 35 MINUTES   MAKES 4 MAIN-DISH SERVINGS.

2 to 3 small red potatoes (6 1/2 ounces)
1 tablespoon olive oil
1 1/2 cups thinly sliced onions
1 zucchini (6 ounces), thinly sliced
1 cup thinly sliced cremini
  mushrooms
2 plum tomatoes (6 1/2 ounces),
  cored, halved, and thinly sliced
1/2 teaspoon kosher salt (optional)
1/2 teaspoon freshly ground black
  pepper
1 cup shredded spinach or Swiss
  chard

1 tablespoon slivered fresh basil
  leaves (optional)
2 large eggs
3 large egg whites
3 tablespoons crumbled feta cheese
  (optional)
2 tablespoons chopped fresh flat-leaf
  parsley
3/4 cup bottled salsa
4 (6-inch) corn tortillas
1/2 jicama (8 ounces), peeled and cut
  into 2" by 1/4" matchstick strips
2 teaspoons fresh lime juice

1. Preheat oven to 350°F. In saucepan, heat potatoes and enough water to cover to a boil over high heat. Reduce heat to low; cover and simmer until fork-tender, 15 to 20 minutes. Drain and cool. Cut into 1/4-inch-thick slices.

2. In nonstick 10-inch oven-safe skillet, heat oil over medium heat. (Wrap handle of skillet with double layer of foil if handle is not oven-safe.) Add onions and cook until softened, about 5 minutes. Add potatoes, zucchini, mushrooms, and tomatoes; cook, stirring gently, until zucchini begins to soften, 2 to 3 minutes. Season with salt, if using, and pepper. Add spinach and basil, if using, and cook until spinach wilts, 1 to 2 minutes.

3. In medium bowl with wire whisk or fork, mix eggs and egg whites. With spatula, stir vegetables while pouring eggs into skillet. Transfer skillet to oven and bake until eggs are set, 3 to 5 minutes.

4. Sprinkle frittata with feta cheese, if using, and parsley. Cut frittata into 4 pieces and serve with salsa, tortillas, and jicama sticks sprinkled with lime juice.

Each serving: About 265 calories (24 percent calories from fat), 11g protein, 38g carbohydrate, 7g total fat (1g saturated), 106mg cholesterol, 140mg sodium.

Vegetarian Tortilla Pie

This dish can be assembled in a jiffy, thanks to its no-cook filling of canned black beans and corn, prepared salsa, and pre-shredded Monterey Jack cheese.

PREP: 8 MINUTES BAKE: 10 MINUTES MAKES 4 MAIN-DISH SERVINGS.

1 jar (12 ounces) medium salsa
1 can (8 ounces) no-salt-added
 tomato sauce
1 can (15 to 16 ounces) no-salt-
 added black beans, rinsed and
 drained
1 can (15 1/4 ounces) no-salt-added
 whole-kernel corn, drained

1/2 cup packed fresh cilantro leaves
4 (10-inch) low-fat flour tortillas
6 ounces reduced-fat Monterey Jack
 cheese, shredded (1 1/2 cups)
reduced-fat sour cream (optional)

1. Preheat oven to 500°F. Spray 15 1/2" by 10 1/2" jelly-roll pan with non-stick cooking spray.
2. In small bowl, mix salsa and tomato sauce. In medium bowl, mix black beans, corn, and cilantro.
3. Place 1 tortilla in prepared jelly-roll pan. Spread one-third of salsa mixture over tortilla. Top with one-third of bean mixture and one-third of cheese. Repeat layering 2 more times, ending with last tortilla.
4. Bake pie until cheese melts and filling is heated through, 10 to 12 minutes. Serve with reduced-fat sour cream if you like.

Each serving: About 440 calories (23 percent calories from fat), 25g protein, 65g carbohydrate, 11g total fat (5g saturated), 30mg cholesterol, 820mg sodium.

Vegetarian Tortilla Pie

Southwestern Black-Bean Burgers

Southwestern Black-Bean Burgers

To have handy for another meal, make a double batch and freeze the uncooked patties. Defrost for 10 minutes, then cook burgers, turning once, until heated through, about 12 minutes.

PREP: 10 MINUTES   COOK: 6 MINUTES   MAKES 4 MAIN-DISH SERVINGS.

1 can (15 to 19 ounces) black beans, rinsed and drained
2 tablespoons light mayonnaise
1/4 cup packed fresh cilantro leaves, chopped
1 tablespoon plain dried bread crumbs
1/2 teaspoon ground cumin
1/2 teaspoon hot pepper sauce
nonstick cooking spray
1 cup loosely packed sliced lettuce
4 mini (4-inch) whole-wheat pitas, warmed
1/2 cup bottled mild salsa

1. In large bowl, with potato masher or fork, mash beans with mayonnaise until almost smooth (some lumps of beans should remain). Stir in cilantro, bread crumbs, cumin, and pepper sauce until combined. With lightly floured hands, shape bean mixture into four 3-inch round patties. Spray both sides of each patty lightly with nonstick cooking spray.
2. Heat nonstick 12-inch skillet over medium heat. Add patties and cook until lightly browned, about 3 minutes. With wide metal spatula, turn patties over and cook until heated through, 3 minutes longer.
3. Arrange lettuce on pitas; top with burgers, then salsa.

Each serving: About 210 calories (13 percent calories from fat), 13g protein, 42g carbohydrate, 3g total fat (0g saturated), 0mg cholesterol, 715mg sodium.

DESSERTS

Plum Yogurt Pops (page 234)

Oranges with Caramel

Serve as a light and elegant finale to a rich meal. When the caramel-drizzled orange rounds are refrigerated, the caramel melts into a luscious golden syrup.

PREP: 30 MINUTES PLUS CHILLING COOK: 10 MINUTES
MAKES 6 SERVINGS.

6 large navel oranges   **1 cup sugar**
2 tablespoons brandy (optional)

1. From oranges, with vegetable peeler, remove 6 strips (3" by 3/4" each) peel. Cut strips lengthwise into slivers. Cut remaining peel and white pith from oranges. Slice oranges into 1/4-inch-thick rounds and place on deep platter, overlapping slices slightly. Sprinkle with brandy, if desired, and orange peel.

2. In 1 1/2-quart saucepan, cook sugar over medium heat, stirring to dissolve any lumps, until sugar has melted and turned deep amber. Drizzle caramel over orange slices. Cover and refrigerate until caramel melts, about 2 hours.

Each serving: About 208 calories (0 calories from fat), 2g protein, 53g carbohydrate, 0g total fat, 0mg cholesterol, 2mg sodium.

Nutrition Spotlight: Citrus

Looking for some vitamin C? Head to the citrus section! On average, a single piece of citrus fruit has 3 grams of fiber and only about 50 calories. Look for the diminutive clementines, garnet-fleshed blood oranges, funny-looking ugli fruit, bite-size kumquats, generous-size yellow and pink grapefruit—and, of course, the fragrant and flavorful traditional orange. And while a glass of fresh-squeezed OJ is pretty sweet to wake up to, you'll miss out on all that good fiber.

Oranges with Caramel

Strawberries in White Wine

Strawberries in White Wine

Make this simple Italian treat with perfectly ripe, fragrant fruit.

PREP: 10 MINUTES MAKES 4 SERVINGS.

1/3 cup dry white wine, such as
  riesling or sauvignon blanc
2 tablespoons sugar

1 pint strawberries, hulled and each
  cut in half

In small bowl, stir wine and sugar together until sugar has dissolved. Divide strawberries among four goblets. Pour wine mixture over fruit.

Each serving: About 61 calories (0 calories from fat), 0g protein, 12g carbohydrate, 0g total fat, 0mg cholesterol, 2mg sodium.

Peaches in Red Wine

Prepare as directed but substitute 1/3 cup red wine for white wine and 2 cups sliced, peeled peaches (3 to 4 peaches) for strawberries.

Each serving: About 75 calories (0 calories from fat), 1g protein, 16g carbohydrate, 0g total fat, 0mg cholesterol, 1mg sodium.

Nutrition Spotlight: Strawberries

Easy to find all year long, strawberries are at their sweet-juice peak in spring. Delicious and nutritious, 12 medium berries weigh in at 45 calories, 3 grams of fiber, and about 135 percent of the Daily Value for vitamin C.

Fast Baked Apples with Oatmeal Streusel

Cooking apples in the microwave, rather than the regular oven, yields plumper, juicier, less shriveled fruit—and saves a big chunk of time!

PREP: 8 MINUTES MICROWAVE: 12 MINUTES MAKES 4 SERVINGS.

**4 large Rome or Cortland apples
(10 ounces each)**
1/4 cup packed brown sugar
1/4 cup quick-cooking oats, uncooked

2 tablespoons chopped dates
1/2 teaspoon ground cinnamon
2 teaspoons butter or margarine

1. Core apples, cutting out a 1 1/4-inch-diameter cylinder from center of each, almost but not all the way through to bottom. Remove peel about one-third of the way down from top. Place apples in shallow 1 1/2-quart ceramic casserole or 8" by 8" glass baking dish.

2. In small bowl, combine brown sugar, oats, dates, and cinnamon. Fill each cored apple with equal amounts of oat mixture. (Mixture will spill over top of apples.) Place 1/2 teaspoon margarine on top of filling in each apple.

3. Microwave apples, covered, on medium-high until tender, 12 to 14 minutes, turning each apple halfway through cooking time. Spoon cooking liquid from baking dish over apples to serve.

Each serving: About 240 calories (11 percent calories from fat), 2g protein, 54g carbohydrate, 3g total fat (3g saturated), 16mg cholesterol, 12mg sodium.

Fast Baked Apples with Oatmeal Streusel

Flambéed Bananas

Be sure to use dark Jamaican rum in this classic dessert: It gives the bananas an irresistible flavor.

PREP: 5 MINUTES   COOK: 8 MINUTES   MAKES 8 SERVINGS.

3 tablespoons butter or margarine
3/4 cup packed brown sugar
1 tablespoon fresh lemon juice
4 ripe medium bananas, each peeled, cut cross-wise in half, and then lengthwise in half

1/3 cup dark Jamaican rum or brandy
vanilla ice cream (optional)

1. In 12-inch skillet, melt butter over medium heat. Stir in brown sugar and lemon juice. Place bananas in single layer in skillet; cook until just slightly softened, about 2 minutes per side. Reduce heat to low.

2. In 1-quart saucepan, heat rum over low heat. With long match, carefully ignite rum; pour over bananas. Spoon rum over bananas until flames die out. Serve with ice cream, if you like.

Each serving: About 179 calories (25 percent calories from fat), 1g protein, 34g carbohydrate, 5g total fat (3g saturated), 12mg cholesterol, 53mg sodium.

Brown Sugar

Exposure to air causes brown sugar to dry out, but adding a slice of apple or bread to the box will soften it. Because air can get trapped between its coarse crystals, brown sugar should be firmly packed when measured.

Fresh Apple Soufflés

A fresh fruit puree is the base for these little soufflés. So much sophistication and flavor for so few calories.

PREP: 45 MINUTES PLUS COOLING   BAKE: 12 MINUTES
MAKES 6 SERVINGS.

4 cups peeled, cored and coarsely
   chopped apples (4 to 5 medium),
   such as McIntosh or Cortland
1 tablespoon fresh lemon juice
1 tablespoon butter or margarine,
   melted

2 tablespoons plus 1/4 cup sugar
6 large egg whites
1/2 teaspoon cream of tartar
1 teaspoon vanilla extract

1. In nonreactive 2-quart saucepan, combine apples and lemon juice. Cover and cook over medium-high heat until apples are soft, about 10 minutes. Remove cover and cook, stirring occasionally, until almost all liquid has evaporated and apples are reduced to 1 cup, about 10 minutes longer.

2. In blender with center of cover removed to allow steam to escape, or in food processor with knife blade attached, puree apple mixture until smooth. Transfer to large bowl; cool to room temperature.

3. Meanwhile, preheat oven to 425°F. Brush six 6-ounce custard cups or ramekins with melted butter and sprinkle with 2 tablespoons sugar.

4. In large bowl, with mixer at high speed, beat egg whites and cream of tartar until soft peaks form when beaters are lifted. Sprinkle in remaining 1/4 cup sugar, 1 tablespoon at a time, beating until sugar has dissolved. Add vanilla; continue beating until egg whites stand in stiff, glossy peaks when beaters are lifted. With rubber spatula, fold beaten egg whites, one-third at a time, into apple mixture just until blended.

5. Spoon into prepared custard cups. Place cups in jelly-roll pan for easier handling. Bake until soufflés have puffed and begin to brown, 12 to 15 minutes. Serve immediately.

Each serving: About 127 calories, (14 percent calories from fat) 4g protein, 24g carbohydrate, 2g total fat (1g saturated), 5mg cholesterol, 75mg sodium.

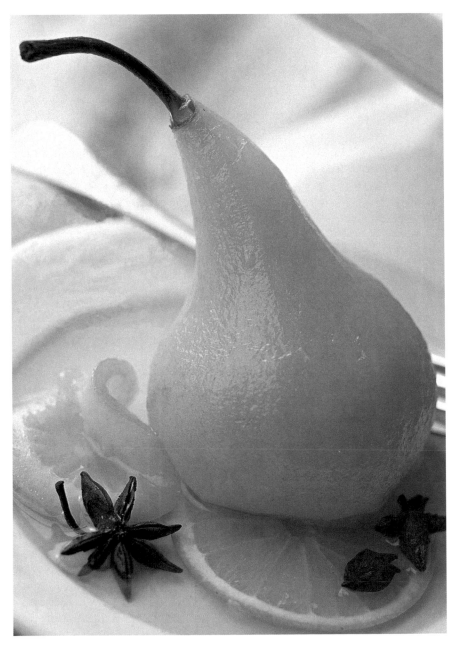

Lemon-Anise Poached Pears

Lemon-Anise Poached Pears

Serve these tender pears and their bracing aromatic syrup in a large glass bowl, and garnish with glistening orange slices.

PREP: 20 MINUTES PLUS CHILLING   COOK: 1 HOUR   MAKES 8 SERVINGS.

1 lemon

8 firm-ripe pears, such as Bosc or Anjou (8 to 9 ounces each), peeled and cored

6 cups water

1 cup sugar

3 whole star anise or 1 teaspoon anise seeds

1 small orange, thinly sliced

1. From lemon, with vegetable peeler, remove 3 strips (3" by 3/4" each) peel; squeeze 2 tablespoons juice. In nonreactive 8-quart saucepot, combine lemon peel, pears, water, sugar, and star anise; heat to boiling over high heat. Reduce heat; cover and simmer until pears are tender, about 30 minutes. With slotted spoon, transfer pears to large bowl. Stir lemon juice into bowl with pears. Strain syrup through sieve into separate large bowl. Return syrup to saucepot.

2. Heat syrup to boiling over high heat; cook, uncovered, until reduced to 3 cups, about 15 minutes. Pour hot syrup over pears. Cover and refrigerate, turning occasionally, until pears are well chilled, at least 6 hours.

3. Serve pears with syrup, garnished with orange slices.

Each serving: About 236 calories (4 percent calories from fat), 1g protein, 61g carbohydrate, 1g total fat (0g saturated), 0mg cholesterol, 1mg sodium.

Pears for Cooking

Bosc and Anjou pears are tops at holding their shape and texture when cooked. In a pinch, Bartletts and other varieties work fine too. Avoid Comice pears for cooking: their tender, juicy flesh tends to fall apart when baked whole or used in pies.

Quick Poached Pears with Ruby-Red Raspberry Sauce

<small>PREP: 10 MINUTES   MICROWAVE: 5 MINUTES   MAKES 2 SERVINGS.</small>

2 medium, ripe Bosc pears
1/2 lemon
2 teaspoons granulated sugar
2 tablespoons water
1 1/2 cups fresh or frozen (thawed) raspberries (reserve 10 raspberries for garnish)

1/3 cup confectioners' sugar
1 tablespoon black currant–flavor or orange-flavor liqueur

1. With melon baller or small knife, remove cores from pears by cutting through blossom end (bottom) of pears. Peel pears almost to top but do not remove stems. Rub pears with lemon half; sprinkle with granulated sugar.

2. In glass pie plate, arrange pears on their sides with stems toward center; add water. Microwave, uncovered, on high until tender, 5 to 6 minutes, turning pears over halfway through cooking. Transfer pears, stem ends up, to 2 dessert plates; set aside until ready to serve.

3. In blender at high speed, puree raspberries. Sift confectioners' sugar through coarse sieve into small bowl. Press raspberry puree through same sieve into same bowl to remove seeds. Discard seeds. Stir liqueur into raspberry mixture.

4. To serve, spoon raspberry sauce over poached pears. Garnish with reserved raspberries.

Each serving: About 245 calories (4 percent calories from fat), 1g protein, 59g carbohydrate, 1g total fat (0g saturated), 0mg cholesterol, 2mg sodium.

Skillet Blueberry Crisps

Homespun and delicious, but easy to stir up in a saucepan!

PREP: 10 MINUTES   COOK: 5 MINUTES   MAKES 4 SERVINGS.

1 medium lemon
1/2 cup cold water
2 tablespoons brown sugar
2 teaspoons cornstarch
2 teaspoons almond-flavor liqueur
1 tablespoon butter or margarine,
  softened

1 pint blueberries
10 amaretti cookies, coarsely
  crushed
confectioners' sugar

1. From lemon, grate 1/4 teaspoon peel and squeeze 1 teaspoon juice. In 2-quart saucepan, combine lemon peel, lemon juice, water, brown sugar, cornstarch, and liqueur. Add margarine and half of blueberries; lightly crush blueberries with potato masher or side of spoon. Bring to a boil over medium heat, stirring constantly. Stir in remaining blueberries and cook, stirring, 2 minutes longer.

2. Spoon hot blueberry mixture into 4 dessert or custard cups; top with cookie crumbs and sprinkle with confectioners' sugar. Serve warm.

Each serving: About 160 calories (23 percent calories from fat), 1g protein, 30g carbohydrate, 4g total fat (2g saturated), 8mg cholesterol, 41mg sodium.

Buying Blueberries

Select purplish-blue to almost black berries with a silvery "bloom" on the outside. Store in the refrigerator covered in the basket for up to ten days or wrap the basket tightly in several layers of plastic wrap and freeze to up to six months. Do not rinse before freezing.

Country Plum Cobbler

Comfort food at its best: fresh, sugared summer plums baked until bubbly, under a golden biscuit crust.

PREP: 20 MINUTES PLUS COOLING BAKE: 50 MINUTES
MAKES 10 SERVINGS.

2 1/2 pounds ripe red or purple plums (about 10 medium), each cut into quarters
1/2 cup sugar
2 tablespoons all-purpose flour
1 3/4 cups reduced-fat all-purpose baking mix
1/4 cup yellow cornmeal
3/4 cup water

1. Preheat oven to 400°F. In large bowl, toss plums with sugar and flour. Spoon plum mixture into shallow 2-quart ceramic or glass baking dish. Cover loosely with foil. Bake until plums are very tender, 30 to 35 minutes.
2. Meanwhile, prepare topping: In medium bowl, stir baking mix, cornmeal, and water just until combined.
3. Remove baking dish from oven. Drop 10 heaping spoonfuls of batter randomly on top of plum mixture. Return cobbler to oven and bake, uncovered, until biscuits are browned and plum mixture is bubbling, 20 to 25 minutes longer. Cool slightly to serve warm, or cool completely to serve later. Reheat if desired.

Each serving: About 190 calories (9 percent calories from fat), 3g protein, 41g carbohydrate, 2g total fat (0g saturated), 0mg cholesterol, 230mg sodium.

Buying Plums

A plum's sweetness does not increase as the fruit softens, so be sure to purchase ripe fruit. Its color is determined by the variety. Plums should be plump and evenly colored and yield to gentle pressure. A powdery bloom on the skin indicates that the plum hasn't been overhandled. Avoid hard, shriveled, or cracked plums.

Country Plum Cobbler

Spicy Plum Compote

Spicy Plum Compote

Plum slices are simmered just long enough in a lemony–allspice syrup to give them a hint of exotic flavor.

Prep: 10 minutes plus chilling   Cook: 6 minutes
Makes 4 servings.

1/2 cup sugar
3 strips lemon peel (3" by 1/2" each)
4 whole allspice berries
2 cups water
4 ripe medium red, purple, and/or
   green plums (1 pound), cut into
   1/2-inch slices

1/2 teaspoon vanilla extract
low-fat yogurt (optional)

1. In 2-quart saucepan, combine sugar, lemon peel, allspice, and water; heat to boiling over high heat. Boil 5 minutes.
2. Stir plums into syrup; heat to boiling over high heat. Reduce heat to low; simmer 1 minute or just until plums are tender.
3. Pour mixture into bowl; stir in vanilla. Cover and refrigerate until cold, about 2 hours. Serve with yogurt if you like.

Each serving: About 135 calories (0 calories from fat), 1g protein, 34g carbohydrate, 0g total fat, 0mg cholesterol, 0mg sodium.

Three-Fruit Salad with Vanilla Bean Syrup

Perfect alone but also a delicious accompaniment to pound cake. If you don't have a vanilla bean, stir one-half teaspoon vanilla extract into the chilled syrup.

PREP: 30 MINUTES PLUS CHILLING   COOK: 10 MINUTES
MAKES 12 SERVINGS.

2 large lemons
1 vanilla bean
3/4 cup water
3/4 cup sugar
3 ripe mangoes, peeled and cut into
   1-inch pieces

2 pints strawberries, hulled and each
   cut in half, or into quarters if large
1 medium honeydew melon, peeled
   and cut into 1-inch pieces

1. From 1 lemon, with vegetable peeler, remove 1-inch-wide continuous strip of peel; from lemons, squeeze 1/4 cup juice. Cut vanilla bean lengthwise in half. With small knife, scrape seeds from vanilla bean; reserve seeds and pod.
2. In 1-quart saucepan, combine lemon peel, vanilla-bean seeds and pod, water, and sugar; heat to boiling over high heat. Reduce heat to medium and cook until syrup has thickened slightly, about 5 minutes. Pour syrup mixture through sieve into small bowl; stir in lemon juice. Cover and refrigerate syrup until chilled, about 2 hours.
3. Place mangoes, strawberries, and melon in large bowl; add syrup and toss.

Each serving: About 138 calories (0 calories from fat), 1g protein, 35g carbohydrate, 0g total fat, 0mg cholesterol, 13mg sodium.

Orange Sherbet

No need to pull out your ice-cream machine for this rich and creamy sorbet.

PREP: 10 MINUTES PLUS CHILLING AND FREEZING COOK: 10 MINUTES
MAKES ABOUT 4 CUPS OR 8 SERVINGS.

1 ¹/₂ cups milk	**5 large oranges**
¹/₂ cup sugar	**¹/₈ teaspoon salt**

1. In heavy 2-quart saucepan, combine milk and sugar; cook over medium-high heat, stirring occasionally, until bubbles form around edge and sugar has completely dissolved, about 2 minutes. Pour into medium bowl; press plastic wrap onto surface. Refrigerate until well chilled, about 1 hour or up to 4 hours.

2. From oranges, grate 1 teaspoon peel and squeeze 2 cups juice. Stir orange peel, orange juice, and salt into chilled milk mixture. Pour into 9-inch square metal baking pan; cover and freeze until firm, at least 4 hours.

3. With spoon, scoop sherbet into food processor with knife blade attached. Process sherbet until smooth but still frozen. Return mixture to pan; cover and freeze until firm, 1 to 2 hours longer.

4. To serve, let sherbet stand at room temperature until just soft enough to scoop, about 10 minutes.

Each serving: About 104 calories (17 percent calories from fat), 2g protein, 21g carbohydrate, 2g total fat (1g saturated), 6mg cholesterol, 60mg sodium.

Plum Yogurt Pops

Forget store-bought popsicles: This super-fruity refresher will be a cool hit with kids of all ages. Make a day in advance to allow enough time for freezing.

PREP: 15 MINUTES PLUS FREEZING   MAKES 16 POPS.

1 pound ripe red or purple plums
  (4 medium), coarsely chopped
1/2 cup sugar

1 tablespoon fresh lemon juice
2 cups vanilla low-fat yogurt

1. In blender, at medium speed, puree plums, sugar, and lemon juice. Pour plum puree into medium-mesh sieve set over medium bowl. With spoon, press purée against sieve to push through pulp and juice. Discard solids in sieve.

2. With wire whisk, mix yogurt and plum mixture until well combined.

3. Spoon yogurt mixture into sixteen 3-ounce paper cups; freeze 4 hours or until partially frozen. Insert wooden ice-cream-bar sticks and freeze until completely frozen. (Or, spoon yogurt mixture into sixteen 2-ounce popsicle molds; seal and insert wooden sticks as manufacturer directs. Freeze overnight.)

Each pop: About 60 calories (15 percent calories from fat), 1g protein, 13g carbohydrate, 1g total fat (0g saturated), 2mg cholesterol, 20mg sodium.

Plum Yogurt Pops

Peach Granita

Be sure the peaches or nectarines are as ripe as possible.

PREP: 20 MINUTES PLUS FREEZING MAKES ABOUT 8 CUPS OR 16 SERVINGS.

1 cup sugar
1 1/4 cups water

1 3/4 pounds peaches or nectarines
   (5 medium), unpeeled and cut into
   wedges
2 tablespoons fresh lemon juice

1. In 1-quart saucepan, heat sugar and water to boiling over high heat, stirring occasionally. Reduce heat to medium; cook mixture about 1 minute or until sugar dissolves completely. Transfer to small bowl to cool.

2. In blender, at medium speed, blend unpeeled peach wedges until smooth. Pour puree into medium-mesh sieve set over medium bowl. With spoon, press puree against sieve to push through pulp and juice. You should have 3 cups puree; discard solids in sieve.

3. Stir sugar syrup and lemon juice into puree. Pour peach mixture into 9" by 9" metal baking pan.

4. Cover with foil or plastic wrap. Freeze until partially frozen, about 2 hours; stir with fork. Freeze until completely frozen, at least 3 hours or overnight.

5. To serve, let granita stand at room temperature until softened slightly, about 15 minutes. With spoon or fork, scrape across surface of granita to create pebbly texture.

Each serving: About 65 calories (0 calories from fat), 0g protein, 17g carbohydrate, 0g total fat, 0mg cholesterol, 0mg sodium.

Blueberry Granita

Prepare as directed but substitute 3 pints blueberries for the peaches.

Each serving: About 80 calories (0 calories from fat), 0g protein, 20g carbohydrate, 0g total fat, 0mg cholesterol, 5mg sodium.

Raspberry Granita

Prepare as directed but substitute 6 half-pints raspberries for the peaches and 2 tablespoons lime juice for the lemon juice.

Each serving: About 70 calories (0 calories from fat), 0g protein, 18g carbohydrate, 0g total fat, 0mg cholesterol, 0mg sodium.

Watermelon Granita

Prepare as directed but substitute 1 piece (5½ pounds) watermelon, seeded and cut into chunks, for the peaches, 2 tablespoons lime juice for the lemon juice, and decrease the water to ³/₄ cup.

Each serving: About 70 calories (0 calories from fat), 1g protein, 17g carbohydrate, 0g total fat, 0mg cholesterol, 2mg sodium.

Banana–Maple Sorbet

Banana-Maple Sorbet

Here's what to do with very ripe bananas—just freeze them, then buzz in the food processor.

Prep: 5 minutes plus freezing   Makes about 3 cups or 6 servings.

4 very ripe medium bananas
1/3 cup maple syrup

1 teaspoon vanilla extract
pinch salt

1. Peel bananas and place in large self-sealing plastic bag; freeze overnight or until very firm.

2. Slice frozen bananas. In food processor with knife blade attached, process bananas, syrup, vanilla, and salt until creamy, about 2 minutes. Serve immediately.

Each serving: About 115 calories (0 calories from fat), 1g protein, 29g carbohydrate, 0g total fat, 0mg cholesterol, 25mg sodium.

Buying Maple Syrup

Pure maple syrup is graded by color, which can range from pale brownish-gold to an almost molasses hue. A syrup's color is affected by climate, when the sap was harvested, and how long the sap was stored. A good rule of thumb: The darker the color, the heartier and more robust the flavor. Vermont Fancy or U.S. Grade A Light Amber is mild and tastes best with foods that won't overpower its sweet, subtle flavor. U.S. Grade A Medium Amber and U.S. Grade A Dark Amber have a stronger taste and aroma and pair well with breakfast waffles and pancakes. Grade A Medium is the type most often found on store shelves. U.S. Grade B has an intense flavor that can stand up to the heat of cooking.

Frozen Chocolate Kahlúa Mousse

When company's coming unexpectedly, or you need a special dessert at the last minute, this delicate, rich-tasting confection rises to the occasion—and it's fat-free, to boot.

PREP: 10 MINUTES PLUS FREEZING MAKES 6 SERVINGS.

1 envelope unflavored gelatin	6 tablespoons sugar
1 cup cold water	1/2 cup Kahlúa liqueur
1/2 cup nonfat ricotta cheese	3 tablespoons unsweetened cocoa
1/2 cup cold fat-free (skim) milk	pinch salt

1. In 1-quart saucepan, evenly sprinkle gelatin over cold water; let stand 2 minutes to soften gelatin slightly. Cook over medium heat, stirring frequently, until gelatin has completely dissolved (do not boil).

2. In blender, combine gelatin mixture, ricotta, milk, sugar, liqueur, and cocoa. Blend until smooth, about 1 minute. Pour into dessert glasses and freeze at least 2 hours.

Each serving: About 100 calories (0 calories from fat), 5g protein, 16g carbohydrate, 0g total fat, 3mg cholesterol, 80mg sodium.

Nutrition Spotlight: Chocolate

The darker the chocolate, the better it is for you. Bittersweet chocolate is rich in flavonols that have been found to reduce blood pressure and LDL cholesterol (the "bad" kind).

Butterscotch Blondies

These chewy treats are one of our test kitchen's favorites—it's hard to believe there's only three grams of fat in each one!

PREP: 15 MINUTES BAKE: 35 MINUTES MAKES 16 BLONDIES.

1 cup all-purpose flour
1/2 teaspoon baking powder
1/4 teaspoon salt
3 tablespoons butter or margarine
3/4 cup packed dark brown sugar

2 large egg whites
1/3 cup dark corn syrup
2 teaspoons vanilla extract
2 tablespoons finely chopped pecans

1. Preheat oven to 350°F. Grease 8-inch square baking pan. In bowl, combine flour, baking powder, and salt.

2. In large bowl, with mixer at medium speed, beat butter and brown sugar until well blended, about 2 minutes. Reduce speed to low; beat in egg whites, corn syrup, and vanilla until smooth. Beat in flour mixture just until combined. Spread batter evenly in prepared pan. Sprinkle with pecans.

3. Bake until toothpick inserted in center comes out clean and edges are lightly browned, 35 to 40 minutes. Cool completely in pan on wire rack.

4. When cool, cut into 4 strips, then cut each strip crosswise into 4 pieces.

Each blondie: About 117 calories (23 percent calories from fat), 1g protein, 21g carbohydrate, 3g total fat (1g saturated), 6mg cholesterol, 94mg sodium.

Fudgy Brownies

Moist, chocolaty, and low-fat. Need we say more? Serve with cold skim milk for a healthful and delicious treat.

PREP: 15 MINUTES BAKE: 18 MINUTES MAKES 16 BROWNIES.

1 teaspoon instant espresso-coffee powder
1 teaspoon hot water
3/4 cup all-purpose flour
1/2 cup unsweetened cocoa
1/2 teaspoon baking powder
1/4 teaspoon salt
3 tablespoons butter or margarine
3/4 cup sugar
2 large egg whites
1/4 cup dark corn syrup
1 teaspoon vanilla extract

1. Preheat oven to 350°F. Grease 8-inch square baking pan. In cup, dissolve espresso powder in hot water; set aside. In large bowl, combine flour, cocoa, baking powder, and salt.

2. In 2-quart saucepan, melt butter over low heat. Remove from heat. With wooden spoon, stir in espresso, sugar, egg whites, corn syrup, and vanilla until blended. Stir sugar mixture into flour mixture just until blended (do not overmix). Pour batter into prepared pan.

3. Bake until toothpick inserted in center comes out almost clean, 18 to 22 minutes. Cool brownies completely in pan on wire rack.

4. When cool, cut brownies into 4 strips, then cut each strip crosswise into 4 pieces. If brownies are difficult to cut, use knife dipped in hot water and dried; repeat as necessary.

Each brownie: About 103 calories (26 percent calories from fat), 2g protein, 19g carbohydrate, 3g total fat (2g saturated), 6mg cholesterol, 88mg sodium.

Date Bars

These beloved triple-layer sweets have a simple streusel topping.

PREP: 40 MINUTES PLUS COOLING   BAKE: 45 MINUTES   MAKES 12 BARS.

OAT CRUST AND TOPPING
1 1/4 cups all-purpose flour
1 cup old-fashioned or quick-cooking
   oats, uncooked
1/2 cup packed light brown sugar
1/2 cup butter (1 stick), softened
1/4 teaspoon baking soda
1/4 teaspoon ground cinnamon
1/4 teaspoon salt

DATE FILLING
1 container (10 ounces) pitted dates,
   chopped
3/4 cup water
2 tablespoons light brown sugar

1. Preheat oven to 375°F. Grease 9" by 9" metal baking pan. Line pan with foil; grease foil.

2. Prepare crust and topping: In large bowl, with hand, mix flour, oats, brown sugar, butter, baking soda, cinnamon, and salt until mixture comes together. Transfer 2 cups mixture to prepared baking pan; reserve remaining mixture for crumb topping. With hand, press mixture evenly onto bottom of pan to form a crust. Bake crust 10 minutes. Cool completely in pan on wire rack. Turn off oven.

3. While crust is cooling, prepare filling: In 2-quart saucepan, combine dates, water, and brown sugar. Cook over medium heat, stirring frequently, until mixture thickens and all liquid is absorbed, 6 to 8 minutes. Spoon filling into bowl and refrigerate until cool, about 30 minutes.

4. When filling is cool, preheat oven to 375°F. Spread filling over crust; top with reserved crumb mixture. Bake until topping is golden, 35 to 40 minutes. Cool completely in pan on wire rack.

5. When cool, transfer with foil to cutting board and remove foil. Cut into 4 strips, then cut each strip crosswise into 3 pieces.

Each bar: About 275 calories (29 percent calories from fat), 4g protein, 47g carbohydrate, 9g total fat (5g saturated), 21mg cholesterol, 155mg sodium.

Ricotta-Cheese Cookies

These soft, Italian-style cookies will be a hit with everyone. The baked cookies freeze well.

PREP: 30 MINUTES PLUS COOLING   BAKE: 15 MINUTES PER BATCH
MAKES ABOUT 72 COOKIES.

2 cups sugar
1 cup margarine or butter (2 sticks), softened
1 container (15 ounces) ricotta cheese
2 teaspoons vanilla extract
2 large eggs

4 cups all-purpose flour
2 tablespoons baking powder
1 teaspoon salt
1 1/2 cups confectioners' sugar
3 tablespoons milk
red and green sugar crystals

1. Preheat oven to 350°F. In large bowl, with mixer at low speed, beat sugar and margarine until blended. Increase speed to high; beat until light and fluffy, about 5 minutes. At medium speed, beat in ricotta, vanilla, and eggs until well combined.

2. Reduce speed to low. Add flour, baking powder, and salt; beat until a dough forms.

3. Drop dough by level tablespoons, 2 inches apart, onto ungreased large cookie sheet. Bake until cookies are very lightly golden (they will be soft), about 15 minutes. With pancake turner, transfer cookies to wire rack to cool. Repeat with remaining dough.

4. When cookies are cool, prepare icing: In small bowl, stir confectioners' sugar and milk until smooth. With small metal spatula or knife, spread icing on cookies; sprinkle with red or green sugar crystals. Set cookies aside to allow icing to dry completely, about 1 hour.

Each cookie: About 90 calories (30 percent calories from fat), 1g protein, 14g carbohydrate, 3g total fat (1g saturated), 3mg cholesterol, 100mg sodium.

Oatmeal-Raisin Cookies

If you thought the words "delicious" and "low-fat" could never be used to describe the same cookie, think again. This one's chewy and sweet, yet it has only two grams of fat per cookie.

Prep: 15 minutes Bake: 10 minutes per batch
Makes about 48 cookies.

2 cups all-purpose flour
1 teaspoon baking soda
1/2 teaspoon salt
1/2 cup light corn-oil spread (1 stick),
  56 to 60% fat
3/4 cup packed dark brown sugar

1/2 cup granulated sugar
2 large egg whites
1 large egg
2 teaspoons vanilla extract
1 cup quick-cooking oats, uncooked
1/2 cup dark seedless raisins

1. Preheat oven to 375°F. Grease two large cookie sheets. In medium bowl, combine flour, baking soda, and salt.

2. In large bowl, with mixer at low speed, beat corn-oil spread and brown and granulated sugars until well combined. Increase speed to high; beat until mixture is light and fluffy. Add egg whites, whole egg, and vanilla; beat until blended. With wooden spoon, stir in flour mixture, oats, and raisins until combined.

3. Drop dough by level tablespoons, 2 inches apart, on prepared cookie sheets. Bake until golden, 10 to 12 minutes, rotating cookie sheets between upper and lower oven racks halfway through baking. With wide spatula, transfer cookies to wire racks to cool completely.

4. Repeat with remaining dough.

Each cookie: About 67 calories (27 percent calories from fat), 1g protein, 12g carbohydrate, 2g total fat (0g saturated), 4mg cholesterol, 72mg sodium.

INDEX

PHOTOGRAPHY CREDITS

Page 2: Brian Hagiwara **Page 8:** Brian Hagiwara **Page 17:** Brian Hagiwara **Page 19:** Brian Hagiwara **Page 24:** Brian Hagiwara **Page 29:** Brian Hagiwara **Page 33:** Jonelle Weaver **Page 36:** Rita Maas **Page 39:** Rita Maas **Page 43:** Jonelle Weaver **Page 45:** Rita Maas **Page 53:** Alan Richardson **Page 56:** Mark Thomas **Page 61:** Brian Hagiwara **Page 67:** Ann Stratton **Page 71:** Ann Stratton **Page 75:** Mark Thomas **Page 78:** Ann Stratton **Page 80:** Ann Stratton **Page 85:** Beatriz da Costa **Page 88:** Alan Richardson **Page 93:** courtesy of Good Housekeeping **Page 94:** Brian Hagiwara **Page 97:** Ann Stratton **Page 102:** Mark Thomas **Page 106:** Mark Thomas **Page 109:** Steven Mark Needham **Page 110:** Mark Thomas **Page 113:** Mark Thomas **Page 114:** Brian Hagiwara **Page 120:** Mark Thomas **Page 125:** Alan Richardson **Page 129:** Brian Hagiwara **Page 131:** Mark Thomas **Page 137:** Alan Richardson **Page 140:** Mark Thomas **Page 143:** Mark Thomas **Page 149:** Mark Thomas **Page 151:** Zeva Oelbaum **Page 157:** Martin Jacobs **Page 158:** Brian Hagiwara **Page 167:** Charles Gold **Page 169:** Brian Hagiwara **Page 173:** Brian Hagiwara **Page 174:** Brian Hagiwara **Page 177:** Brian Hagiwara **Page 180:** Brian Hagiwara **Page 184:** Brian Hagiwara **Page 193:** Brian Hagiwara **Page 198:** Brian Hagiwara **Page 201:** Rita Maas **Page 204:** Steven Mark Needham **Page 211:** Brian Hagiwara **Page 212:** Brian Hagiwara **Page 237:** Brian Hagiwara

METRIC CONVERSION CHARTS

The recipes that appear in this cookbook use the standard United States method for measuring liquid and dry or solid ingredients (teaspoons, tablespoons, and cups). The information on this chart is provided to help cooks outside the U.S. successfully use these recipes. All equivalents are approximate.

METRIC EQUIVALENTS FOR DIFFERENT TYPES OF INGREDIENTS

A standard cup measure of a dry or solid ingredient will vary in weight depending on the type of ingredient. A standard cup of liquid is the same volume for any type of liquid. Use the following chart when converting standard cup measures to grams (weight) or milliliters (volume).

Standard Cup	Fine Powder (e.g., flour)	Grain (e.g., rice)	Granular (e.g., sugar)	Liquid Solids (e.g., butter)	Liquid (e.g., milk)
1	140 g	150 g	190 g	200 g	240 ml
$3/4$	105 g	113 g	143 g	150 g	180 ml
$2/3$	93 g	100 g	125 g	133 g	160 ml
$1/2$	70 g	75 g	95 g	100 g	120 ml
$1/3$	47 g	50 g	63 g	67 g	80 ml
$1/4$	35 g	38 g	48 g	50 g	60 ml
$1/8$	18 g	19 g	24 g	25 g	30 ml

USEFUL EQUIVALENTS FOR LIQUID INGREDIENTS BY VOLUME

$1/4$ tsp =				1 ml
$1/2$ tsp =				2 ml
1 tsp =				5 ml
3 tsp =	1 tbls =		$1/2$ fl oz =	15 ml
	2 tbls =	$1/8$ cup =	1 fl oz =	30 ml
	4 tbls =	$1/4$ cup =	2 fl oz =	60 ml
	$5 1/3$ tbls =	$1/3$ cup =	3 fl oz =	80 ml
	8 tbls =	$1/2$ cup =	4 fl oz =	120 ml
	$10 2/3$ tbls =	$2/3$ cup =	5 fl oz =	160 ml
	12 tbls =	$3/4$ cup =	6 fl oz =	180 ml
	16 tbls =	1 cup =	8 fl oz =	240 ml
	1 pt =	2 cups =	16 fl oz =	480 ml
	1 qt =	4 cups =	32 fl oz =	960 ml
			33 fl oz =	1000 ml = 1l

USEFUL EQUIVALENTS FOR DRY INGREDIENTS BY WEIGHT

(To convert ounces to grams, multiply the number of ounces by 30.)

1 oz =	$1/16$ lb =	30 g
4 oz =	$1/4$ lb =	120 g
8 oz =	$1/2$ lb =	240 g
12 oz =	$3/4$ lb =	360 g
16 oz =	1 lb =	480 g

USEFUL EQUIVALENTS FOR COOKING/OVEN TEMPERATURES

	Fahrenheit	Celsius	Gas Mark
Freeze Water	32° F	0° C	
Room Temperature	68° F	20° C	
Boil Water	212° F	100° C	
Bake	325° F	160° C	3
	350° F	180° C	4
	375° F	190° C	5
	400° F	200° C	6
	425° F	220° C	7
	450° F	230° C	8
Broil			Grill

USEFUL EQUIVALENTS FOR LENGTH

(To convert inches to centimeters, multiply the number of inches by 2.5.)

1 in =		2.5 cm
6 in =	$1/2$ ft =	15 cm
12 in =	1 ft =	30 cm
36 in =	3 ft = 1 yd =	90 cm
40 in =		100 cm = 1 m